12/20

CITY
ON THE
EDGE

CITY ON THE EDGE

HARD CHOICES IN THE AMERICAN RUST BELT

MICHAEL STREISSGUTH

excelsior editions

AN IMPRINT OF STATE UNIVERSITY OF NEW YORK PRESS
www.sunypress.edu

Cover: The State Tower building in Syracuse.
Photograph © 2020 Jordan Harmon

Published by State University of New York Press, Albany
© 2020 Michael Streissguth
All rights reserved

Printed in the United States of America

Excelsior Editions is an imprint of
State University of New York Press

For information, contact State University
of New York Press, Albany, NY

www.sunypress.edu

Library of Congress Cataloging-in-Publication Data

Names: Streissguth, Michael, 1966– author.
Title: City on the edge : hard choices in the American rust belt /
Michael Streissguth.
Description: Albany : State University of New York Press, 2020. |
Series: Excelsior editions | Includes bibliographical references
and index.
Identifiers: LCCN 2019037042 | ISBN 9781438479903 (paperback)
| ISBN 9781438479897 (ebook)
Subjects: LCSH: Syracuse (N.Y.)—History. | Syracuse (N.Y.)—
Biography. | Syracuse (N.Y.)—Social conditions. | Syracuse
(N.Y.)—Economic conditions. | Deindustrialization—New York—
Syracuse. | Deindustrialization—Lake States—Case studies.
Classification: LCC F129.S8 S733 2020 | DDC 974.7/66—dc23
LC record available at https://lccn.loc.gov/2019037042

10 9 8 7 6 5 4 3 2 1

CONTENTS

ACKNOWLEDGMENTS

More than 20 years ago, my wife and I came to Syracuse with our two-year-old daughter and another daughter six weeks away from delivery. A growing family will help you get to know a community and, sure enough, we met neighbors who were also parents and they introduced us to others around the city. Soon, there were church and nursery school and then elementary school to expand our social circles. The people in our neighborhood, those beguiling West Siders, became our Syracuse.

But even after two decades I really didn't know the half of it. I understood Syracuse community life was great and its mild summers couldn't be beat, and I accepted the irksome things, like unfocused economic development and the ninja motorcyclists who kicked up turf in our city parks. And I still often felt more like a Washingtonian than a Syracusan, resisting the unrelenting snows and never really understanding the allure of salt potatoes. So I wrote this book as a kind of submission to the city, accepting finally that Syracuse blood flowed in my veins.

This deep dive into my adopted hometown revealed the Syracuse Five: Stefon Greene, Elise Baker, Jessi Lyons, Justo Triana, and Neil Murphy. Three years later, I thank them for helping me to better understand how life courses through a city when it can seem to a cynic a static thing. They never shied away from hard questions and gave generously of their time. Much of that time was spent in the city's coffee shops, the real idea incubators in Syracuse, so thanks to Café Kubal, The Broadway Café, and Salt City Coffee.

Early drafts of this book were burdened by my blustery criticism of careless state policies and leadership, local indecision about the future of the I-81 highway, and developers who suck up tax breaks mostly for hotels that do little for economic development. There may still be a book to be written about those plagues, but my subjects didn't really care about them. Instead, they focused on what they—not political leaders—could do as individuals to build a bridge to the future. That was the yellow signal flag they raised in Syracuse, and I feel fortunate to have finally seen it.

My deep gratitude also goes to other interviewees: Debra Mims, Maurice Hoston, Rob Hoston, Trevor Russell, Brandon Baker, and Jasenko Mondom.

So many others have shown me their Syracuse and influenced my thinking about the city. At the top of the list are Edward and Carolyn Brown, with whom my wife, Leslie, and I have spent countless hours discussing urban life and our place in it. And there's Sean Kirst, the city's foremost writer and another coffee partner, whose work at the (Syracuse) *Post-Standard* and the *Buffalo News*, and in numerous books, has helped readers better understand what it means to live in New York's upstate cities, bearing witness to the nobility of this region.

Le Moyne College, my employer for as long as I've lived here, has been another pathway to the city. Earlier in the decade, President Linda Le-Mura, then provost, asked me to be a dean for one year, which pushed me to many forums where the school's and the city's interests intersected, and I've joyfully tracked many former students who have chosen to live and work here. Indeed, Le Moyne—in the shadow of Syracuse University—is a driver in these parts. Thanks also to the college's Research and Development Committee, which approved the sabbatical that allowed me to complete this book.

I'm particularly indebted to Amanda Lanne-Camilli, Jenn Bennett-Genthner, and James Harbeck at SUNY Press, and Dr. Micki Pulleyking, who invited me to the 2018 Public Affairs Conference at Missouri State University, where I met colleagues who were essential to the life of this book.

Many thanks to my neighbors throughout the Strathmore neighborhood. And to Maureen and Ozzie Mocete, Mary Jo and Jim Spano, J. B., Joe Kelly who continued to ask, Fernando Diz who championed "edge" over "moments," Chris and Gretchen Kinnell, Adam Sudmann of My Lucky Tummy, Peter Willner, Fr. Fred Mannara, Sarah and Masih Robin, Jamie Cunningham, Angela Locke and Astrid Choromanska of the West Side Learning Center, Mike Woods, Jay Subedi, Rai Thetika, Naureen Greene, Mike Melara of Catholic Charities of Onondaga County, Sarah Kozma at the Onondaga Historical Association, Steven Featherstone, Wayne Stevens, Dan Roche, Dave Smetters, Phil Novak, Martin Goettsch, Jordan Harmon, Julie Grossman, Bryan Cole, Fr. David McCallum, Jim Hannan, James Joseph, Fr. Joe Marina, Ann Ryan, Kate Costello-Sullivan, Shawn Ward, Farha Ternikar, Josefa Alvarez, Melissa Short, Jeanne Darby, and David Lloyd.

And my eternal thanks to the home team: Leslie, Emily, Cate, and Will.

INTRODUCTION

✧ ✧ ✧

CITY OF
MOMENTS

The gods of the urban epoch grant an American city at least one golden moment, a time when it comes into the light and finally embodies its destiny. Think Boston in the pre–Revolutionary War period, Chicago at the dawn of the twentieth century, and Memphis at the mid-twentieth-century mark, when it lubricated the Mid-South economy and exported blues and rock and roll music to the world. A city in the moment has distilled its gifts—geographic location, natural resources, human intelligence, labor—and joined networks that connect to the nation and beyond, economically and culturally. Without question, "in the moment" is the place to be.

1

A few cities may have more than one moment. New York City exploded in economic and artistic influence in the twentieth century thanks in part to the mass of humanity from Europe that had arrived in its harbor, and it could do so again by addressing hyper-gentrification and global warming's rising waters. In North Carolina, the city of Charlotte lost its textile-fueled moment starting forty years ago, but today it's a national economic and transportation hub with pro sports and multiple colleges and universities, a city in a second moment—though not without flaws—that attracts new residents who can chase their dreams.

Syracuse, New York's moment lasted for more than half a century, 1900 to 1960, an era of incredible economic expansion and population growth that delivered the "Made in Syracuse" tag to almost every home and business in America. Buoyed mostly by an ever-blooming employment market, Pax Siracusa seemed endless. It even communicated a certain mystique, which some current residents might find humorous, accustomed as they are to rutted streets and the untamed brambles that now line the main arteries into town.

But, truthfully, the popular imagination used to see Syracuse in gunmetal glory—reliable, barrel-chested, and tempered by the harsh snows that sweep down from the Great Lakes every winter. Like Duluth, Akron, or Erie, it ranked in the second tier of industrial cities, dwarfed by Pittsburgh, Detroit, and Chicago. But the city projected an everyman spirit, a place where good souls lived. It was home to the historic Erie Canal, a proud immigrant tradition, and blue-collar running backs Ernie Davis and Jim Brown of the 1950s and 1960s racing down the field in a streak of orange, the color of Syracuse University. In the movies, the best friends came from Syracuse, and if the plot hinged on a traveling vaudeville show, chances are the troupe had just finished a good run in that most American of middle-American cities.

Perhaps because the famed Shubert Brothers hailed from Syracuse—they controlled many theaters on Broadway and across the country in the twentieth century—the city often figured prominently in popular plays and musicals. Titles such as *So Was Napoleon* (1930), *The Farmer Takes a Wife* (1934), starring Henry Fonda, and *The 49th Cousin* (1960) were among them.

In Syracuse and beyond, old men in diners still argue about which were the "real cities," meaning those that relied primarily on manufacturing and trade. That is to say any city that wasn't Las Vegas, which sold self-indulgence, or Washington, DC, merely a government town. In their eyes, Syracuse in the mid-twentieth century might have been quintessentially authentic, full of companies exporting their goods to the world and employing flinty people whose wages fueled local economic growth and improved community life.

Rooted in nineteenth-century commerce that burgeoned because of its enviable place at the midpoint of the legendary canal and later on the railroads, Syracuse's red-hot economy churned out a mind-boggling array of products throughout every minute of its shining hour: air conditioners, pharmaceuticals, china, ice cream scoops, auto parts, circuit boards, and furniture. Engines for the immortal Tucker automobiles rode the assembly line just outside the city in the late 1940s while, at the same time, General Electric perfected color television in a local plant. "For generations Syracusans believed that just because they lived in almost the precise center of the state, economic, educational, and cultural benefits would come to them automatically," noted the writer John A. Williams, who grew up in the city during the 1920s and 1930s.[1]

The city nurtured churches, synagogues, fraternal organizations, and athletic clubs. Arts and entertainment flourished, while lush city parks inspired by Frederick Law Olmsted offered Sunday-afternoon respite. It was also home to stately

1. John A. Williams, "Portrait of a City: Syracuse, the Old Home Town," *Syracuse University Library Associates Courier* 28, no. 1 (Spring 1993), http://syracusethenandnow.org/Urban Renewal/Williams/Williams15thWard.htm.

neighborhoods and a nifty American Airlines office where customers purchased tickets at a drive-thru window, not to mention the Syracuse Nationals, one of the National Basketball Association's first powerhouse teams, and Gustav Stickley and Adelaide Robineau, major figures in the Arts and Crafts movement. People flocked to the city from across the nation and all over the world, a destination not unlike Detroit or Oakland, which teemed with newcomers in the post–World War II era.

But by the 1970s the popular imagination had forgotten Syracuse, as it had Duluth, Akron, and Erie. Industry that had nourished families and civic life was hemorrhaging tens of thousands of jobs while a charismatic mayor with two mistresses who were twin sisters larded his bank account with kickbacks from developers drunk on federal urban renewal money. Crumbling infrastructure, soaring poverty rates, and false promises defined the city for the next four decades. When national news media turned to Syracuse, they focused on corruption, racial strife, and plant closings. Things couldn't have been worse in 1986 when a national reporter writing about the city's malaise observed that "a lot of people have never heard of the place."[2]

2. Elizabeth Kolbert, "The Talk of Syracuse: New York's Old 'Salt City' Struggling to Overcome Setbacks," *New York Times,* June 16, 1986.

By the late 1990s, Syracuse had not fully confronted its rust-belt conundrum, unlike Cleveland and Pittsburgh, for example, which had all but lost their heavy manufacturing only to pivot gradually to education and healthcare. Smaller than both cities and therefore potentially nimbler, Syracuse seemed a candidate for rightsizing, consolidating steady strengths in order to find its footing. Could it not exploit the vast water resources in the area in service of a nation fast drying up, or capitalize on its place at the center of a gorgeous natural triangle connecting the Finger Lakes Region, Lake Ontario, and the Adirondack Mountains, or claim its proud progressive tradition dating back to the nineteenth century, when it sheltered fugitive slaves and prominently embraced the women's rights movement?[3] Evidently, the answer was no.

Instead, the city became home to one of the highest concentrations of African American and Hispanic poverty in the nation, the most tragic of rankings because people who live in dense poverty are far less likely to climb out of it. Not surprisingly, then, few from those populations had joined the middle class, as if affirmative action had never existed. Many companies could count on one hand

3. The city hosted no less than a dozen major abolitionist conventions between 1845 and 1850 and was home to Harriet May Mills, a leading suffragist.

their employees of color, and utility crews working for good pay on power lines and cable boxes were virtually all white. One prominent attorney said recently that Syracuse never cared much about finding a place for its people of color in the mainstream of social and economic life, pinpointing what may be the city's tragic flaw.

The list of head-scratching characteristics only seems to grow: de facto racial segregation reigns throughout the region; public transport is minimal; city code enforcement—particularly in housing—lacks teeth;[4] and ruptured pipes, corroded with age, spew up water through the city streets whenever cold weather prevails in this, one of the snowiest urban areas in the contiguous United States.

And city government often resembles a three-ring circus: corrupt police officers have been known to submit bogus timecards and wrangle sexual liaisons with citizens who call for help, while a recent mayor of Syracuse and her counterpart in the county executive's office of Onondaga County, home to the city, nursed an iron-clad grudge that hampered badly needed regional cooperation. One morning in 1999, citizens could have been forgiven if they thought they had woken up in a Robert

---

4. For example, a city law requires residents and business owners to clear their sidewalks after snowstorms but does not levy fines or any other penalty on scofflaws.

Penn Warren novel when the local paper reported that the Onondaga County district attorney, a Republican, had launched a crusade against gossip, pledging to uncover the source of rumors about the Republican mayor's treatment of his wife. Would busybodies chatting over their backyard fences be next? A few years later, that same DA launched an investigation into forged letters of support for the Democratic mayor, a patently trivial matter.

In the midst of all this, the city fell in love with a shopping center, the Carousel Mall. Its owner—developer Robert Congel—had admirably built it on an abandoned oil field in the late 1980s, erasing an eyesore that offended anybody approaching the city from the north. But in 2000, Congel unveiled plans for an expansion of Mall-of-America proportions, proposing indoor golf, a hotel, and a replica of the Erie Canal in exchange for thirty years of tax freedom.

Syracuse contracted a strong case of mall fever. Real estate agents promised rising home values, politicians touted job growth, and the developer prophesied the rejuvenation of the city's fading North Side, which abutted the mall. But the promise was a mirage. A new wing of the mall appeared, but no mega-structure. It would soon come to light that the tax agreement never required Congel to deliver on the totality of his vision. And, in 2020, he still holds his tax breaks. In a word, the city was duped. But the city and the county—through their competing industrial development agencies—remain enamored of tax relief for building projects, mostly hotels that promise little more than low-wage jobs. Like an out-of-control gumball machine, they release enormous handfuls of economic treats when developers deposit a penny.

By Donald J. Trump's inauguration in 2017, you could have called Syracuse a broken city: law enforcement lacked the person-power to respond quickly to 911 calls; city government couldn't pay for repairs to damaged roads; litter covered many sidewalks and exit ramps; drug dealing thrived openly on well-traveled downtown corridors; and violence frequently erupted in the public schools. What's worse, city leaders couldn't point to a new day.

But if not in the moment, Syracuse is still a city of moments, a diverse and magnetic place.

Those who climb to the top of Woodland Reservoir on the southwest side survey a magical scene. In the distance, the university and hospital district gently slopes toward the downtown and then the landscape undulates wherever the eye can see. It's like the Seven Hills of Rome. Beyond the reservoir and around the city, the summits of many ancient drumlins promise astounding views; dozens of neighborhood streets showcase old homes restored to their former grandeur; downtown at sunset reveals quaint alleyways and building façades alive like fire, reflecting the fading light.

Also in the downtown, small, independent businesses have sprung up as if to answer the big mall, that temple of chain stores. Eclectic music halls, farmers markets, bakeries, tiny art galleries, bars selling craft beer, and restaurants pledged to locally sourced food let you know that contemporary movements have come to Syracuse, largely without the mammoth tax breaks that beefy developers enjoy. Repeating a national trend, downtown has also seen a swell of young residents, who have made it the only zip code in the city to see net population growth.

Many families send their children to public schools where fiercely dedicated teachers negotiate dully lit hallways, shortages of textbooks, and sporadic knife fights, but still deliver solid preparation for admission to good universities and career readiness programs. City kids may salivate over the suburban schools' glistening music rooms and national athletic rankings, but the Syracuse schools do their job.

Like anywhere else, schools are the center of wider community life, and community life in Syracuse is rich. Neighbors across the old town gather for block parties and flock to parks for foot races, summer concerts, and annual cleanups. People who live down the street and around the corner become like family members, recommending doctors, watching your children, bringing hot dishes in trying times, meeting up for drinks at a downtown bar. Many are politically active and socially aware, intentional about living in the city, clinging to an urban dream.

Inspiring people who work across social and emergency services populate Syracuse: teachers, volunteer coordinators, directors of non-profits, police officers, counselors, and nurses. They shoulder many of the burdens of this city that time and the national conversation may have forgotten, teaching the illiterate, counseling rape victims, confronting violence on the streets, hunting down shelter for the homeless, treating the drug-addicted, nurturing refugees from war-afflicted nations. They must be resolute in thinking that life can be better in Syracuse, or why would they do what they do with such heart?

Which points to the overriding question of this book. In a city hemorrhaging people and jobs, is there reason to stay? Cities blossom when people in them find purpose, and they wither when they have nothing left to offer. If the city is to discover another moment, then its people must remain to nurture and lead or else it may follow the once great African city of Timbuktu, now slowly melting back into the desert, or the former auto capital of Detroit, popular today among so-called ruin-porn gawkers. For now, many people still make life work in Syracuse. But will the city continue to give them reason to stay?

Five people whose lives are intertwined with the city's help answer that question in this book: Jessi Lyons, an urban farmer attempting to grow community and a local food movement; Neil Murphy Jr., a city elder hellbent for better water management and' smarter government; Elise Baker, an activist and downtown florist whose one and only real concern is the dispossessed; Justo Triana, a hardworking refugee from Cuba who gives as much as he receives by teaching English to fellow refugees; and Stefon Greene, a young man, and the primary figure in this narrative, who almost sank into the city's cruel streets only to bob up again as youth, diversity, and hope personified. Their experiences and perspectives—as they relate them in their own words—plainly and valuably reveal what it's like to live and work in a city on the edge, providing insight into how people discern hope as they decide if a city can remain a sheltering place.

This book strives to give readers a sense of Syracuse as it lives around the five subjects, contextualizing their extended commentary and storytelling with appealing secondary characters and various episodes, such as a tragic Father's Day riot and the trial that followed, sidewalk fistfights, Elise Baker's community-raising convocations, and public debates over a regional consolidation proposal. The narrative also pays particular attention to Stefon Greene's family, who arrived in Syracuse in the late 1940s astride a huge influx of African American people. Representing a seventy-year-long thread, the family's story tracks many of the city's crucial issues: racism, urban renewal, drug abuse, the hope of upward mobility and, most importantly, the question over whether to leave the city or stay, which Stefon must grapple with in 2020.

As Syracusans go, the five commentators in this book are not necessarily unique, but they are thoughtful and quietly energetic, and, like many of their fellow citizens, they help keep the city moving from one day to the next. Framed by a hometown rife with violence, still hobbled by industrial collapse and often narrow in its thinking, they sketch out the city's tragic past and tumultuous present. But in embodying tenacity, innovation, reform and redemption they also propose a vision for Syracuse and for struggling cities everywhere, a rolling path away from oblivion and back into the national sunlight.

1

✧ ✧ ✧

A TRAGIC
FATHER'S DAY

After an unusually hot Father's Day in the city of Syracuse, evening festivities were just getting started at the James Geddes Housing Development near Skiddy Park. About three hundred men, women, and children gathered in the near West Side community while charcoal fires smoked to life and basketballs rolled onto the nearby playground court. Neighbors brought lawn chairs, blankets, beers, and phones for pictures, while at least three men reached for guns in their glove compartments.

As the party grew in the humid night, somebody called 911 about a shooting victim. Such emergencies were stacking up in 2016. So far, the city had clocked fourteen murders on its way to its bloodiest year ever.[1] But when a white Syracuse police officer named Kelsey Francemone arrived at the scene, she found no injuries, only a churning mass, which set off alarm bells in her mind. She called for reinforcements, but cash-strapped Syracuse was more than 100 officers shy of a full force, so help also set out from neighboring towns and villages.

A few minutes later, gunfire startled Francemone, and she watched the revelers run toward their homes and cover. But she charged forward against the frightened tide, spying three men in a parking lot, their guns ablaze. Later, Onondaga County district attorney William Fitzpatrick commented on the "unbelievable amount of firepower" in her midst.[2]

With backup nowhere in sight, the officer barked at the men to drop their guns, but they ignored her. When she fired her own gun, they scattered. She gave chase and apparently tried to fire again, but her weapon jammed. When she stopped to clear it, she turned and saw a black man named Gary Porter firing a handgun. She ordered him to surrender his weapon, but he dashed away and Francemone gave chase. Seconds later, Porter turned toward his side. The DA would later say that he may have been trying to discard his gun, but his motions were all the provocation she needed.[3] The twenty-two-year-old white cop stopped, raised her gun, and shot the forty-one-year-old man in the back. He died soon after at Upstate University Hospital.

The significance was lost on no one: Syracuse had just joined the growing list of cities whose police had shot black men in 2016.

The morning after the Skiddy Park violence, while police investigators combed the ground for clues, Stefon Greene arrived for work at the city's public television station, which sits just a few blocks away from the previous night's melee. One of the city's success stories, the station had pulled up roots in the northern suburb of Liverpool and moved to the splintered near West Side, joining a small renaissance characterized by architecturally adventurous homes, food trucks selling burritos and grilled cheese sandwiches, and the arrival of other nonprofit organizations.

Stefon, a bespectacled producer, is a rarity in Syracuse, which graduates only 60 percent of its children and sees many of its young black men on the

3. House, "DA."

streets, hustling and selling drugs. Born in 1988, he completed high school, finished a degree in communication and film studies at nearby Le Moyne College, and found work in the professional ranks soon after graduation. At a station in a city that is more than 30 percent African American, he is the only black man among approximately fifty employees.

Raised around the chaos of his parents' addiction, he sold drugs for a time, dabbled in other petty crime, and drifted through much of his elementary and secondary school years. His innate smarts and the intervention of concerned relatives and teachers snapped him back from the grim network of Syracuse streets—but not before he had discerned the life lessons around him, including how to act when the cops show up.

He could have told Gary Porter that brandishing a weapon with a cop over his shoulder was definitely not in the playbook. You had to stay calm in the face of police presence even if you'd done nothing wrong. No matter how rude the cop. Despite the anger boiling up inside you. Like when he and Naureen, his prom date (and later his wife), were pulled over on their way to the big high school dance. A cop saw a narrative that matched one of the scripts in his binder: a black man in a tuxedo, driving a white Jaguar, which Stefon had borrowed from his father. The officer approached the vehicle, leaned toward the open window, and asked if Naureen were a prostitute.

Recent national news stories about police shooting black motorists had driven home the lessons learned: stay cool, stay still. To this day, when Stefon heads to the car in the morning, Naureen tells him to buckle up, watch the speed limit, stop at the stop signs. In other words, don't give them a reason to pull you over. "We don't need any police contact," she'll say. Nonetheless, this college-educated, fully employed professional still stumbles into law enforcement's maelstrom, a function of his race and his strong ties to the streets that still shape the lives of friends and family all around him.

"Last summer Naureen's sister had a falling out with her husband," explained Stefon. "He pushed his way into their house and grabbed their baby and had the baby in his car by the time the police got there. So the police let him take him but what was surprising was when we got there—and I work in television now, I've graduated from Le Moyne— the first thing the cop says to me, 'OK. We don't need any of that stuff. Calm down.' I hadn't said anything!

"When the police went into the house, there was a knife on the kitchen counter. They took her to jail for that. The husband told the cop, 'She threatened me with a knife.' But she didn't have it in her hand. When we were trying to talk him out of arresting her, the cop completely loses it. He says, 'We don't have to explain anything. If you don't get out of my face, I'm taking you to jail.'

"Then he said, 'You're making me nervous.' Then Naureen pulls out her phone and starts recording and she says, 'Nope. Stop talking to him, Stefon. Because the next thing you know he'll be fearing for his life.' That was pretty bad because they were pretty blatantly thinking that we were down there to cause a whole bunch of trouble. But we were just trying to find out what was going on. What made me upset was that I was trying to explain to the cop that her husband wasn't a good guy, and that taking her to jail is going to cause a whole bunch of problems down the line that he won't have anything to do with. And it did. It was months of going to court. At one point, they couldn't even find him or the baby. He was threatening to move to New York City and he didn't have a job, a lot of things the judge ended up realizing because the cops on the scene wouldn't listen to us."

In the television station offices, Stefon and his co-workers were summoned to a meeting about the previous evening's fracas. The station manager was assuring his staff that police were in control of the scene, but Stefon fidgeted, not sure that anybody understood the culture in the station's backyard. A few comments shared around the table confirmed his suspicions.

After one man compared Skiddy Park to a war zone, Stefon raised up. "It's not a war zone," he protested. "People live there. That's not changing the kids that live there and go to school there every day and the kids that go to that park just to have fun. And it's not changing the fact that this was a Father's Day cookout. It's a community event and people were just going there to have fun. Can you stop the knuckleheads that are in these places? You can't . . . because they live there, too."

Later, Stefon wondered how the room had perceived him at the meeting, if at all. "Everybody knows a little about my background. They know I'm born and raised in Syracuse, but they don't know the extent of my background and the experiences that I've had with the police. Do I get worried if I get pulled over? Yeah, I get really worried. That's been my whole life. I've never, ever been pulled over by a cop where I wasn't talked to a certain kind of way. I've never not been asked if I had a warrant. They always ask me if I have something illegal in the car. Which is always surprising. When those things happen, it's profiling. But a lot of that is training. It's cops trained under other cops. They tell them, 'Well this is what I do when I'm on the street and this is what you look for.' Those are the wrong things, but I can't blame any one particular cop for being like that.

"Syracuse is a really divided kind of community. There's no way of getting around it. Most everybody at the TV station commutes from these suburban communities. Everybody travels so far that they are totally disconnected with what's going on in the near West Side in this building that they built to benefit the near West Side. In the meeting, I think they were more or less putting out the message that we're safe working here. They don't want people to panic. When you start talking about rioting, start talking about police shootings, especially black men getting shot and people rioting, people get worried."

Despite Stefon's fraught encounters with police, he's certain about Syracuse's irresistible lure. The city is home to his family, his broad network of friends, and his job. The sprawling housing complexes, glistening fountains, and even the weed-filled lots tell the story of his childhood and remind him of people who have come and gone from his life. In recent years, his loyalty to the city has preoccupied him. How could he leave like so many others, effectively communicating to friends and neighbors that you can't succeed in Syracuse?

Yet he thinks daily about leaving. A budding producer and aspiring filmmaker, he dreams of New York City or Los Angeles. Sooner or later, his dreams will butt up against the city's ever-contracting barriers. Over the past four decades, almost all Syracuse natives—including native suburbanites—have wrestled with the same dilemma: cling to the city's shrunken bosom or leave to find professional fulfillment somewhere else. Mostly, Syracuse loses those battles of the heart and mind.

It wasn't always this way. When Stefon's grandparents—Ted and Willa Hoston—arrived from South Bend, Indiana, in the late 1940s, Syracuse was the obvious choice. Big factories, many of them located just north of the city, employed thousands of people. And thousands more worked for smaller manufacturers that had churned out candles, shoes, boilers, beer, and gloves ever since the mid-nineteenth century and the opening of the Erie Canal. If cities exist to create wealth for its citizens then Syracuse was a restless engine. Major companies such as Bristol-Myers, Lockheed Martin, General Electric, and Crucible Steel produced goods in a white-hot frenzy, driving the city's post-war economy. General Electric alone employed 19,000 workers.

Ted was from North Carolina, where his parents had owned a general store. According to family lore, he got mixed up in a gunfight and fled to South Bend, where he repaired and shined shoes in his own little shop. After serving in the army during the Second World War, he returned to his northern Indiana home and met Willa, who already had two children from previous relationships: James (whom she had put up for adoption) and Maurice. Willa herself had been put up for adoption by her mother after her father died in 1930, so Ted's appearance brought some stability to her life. By 1945, they had married.

Ted and Willa's drive to Syracuse took them through Toledo, Cleveland, Erie, and Buffalo, the heartland of American industry. They could have pulled over in any one of those cities and found work, at least for Ted. But, for unknown reasons, they pressed on to Syracuse.

Carrying Maurice with them, Ted and Willa saw glowing smoke stacks and drew back at the acrid smell of soda ash production, which was slowly poisoning the city's Onondaga Lake. Twice a day, trains roared down the streets of the city center. It was otherworldly.

The Hostons headed directly to the 15th Ward, a shabby black neighborhood near downtown, immediately northwest of Syracuse University. In earlier times, the area had been home to many of the city's Jewish people, but they had moved farther east, making way for the growing population of black people who had migrated from the South and other points in recent years. In 1948, when the Hostons first turned up in the city directory, it was the undisputed center of black Syracuse. Ted was listed as a stock clerk.

They rented an apartment at 603 Washington Street and sent their kids to Washington Irving School on Harrison Street. "We lived right next door to a saloon," said Maurice Hoston, Stefon's uncle. "I can remember laying in bed and hearing honky-tonk blues and all that stuff coming from the joint next door. Then I would have the radio going and we had country and western on that. So I was getting a dose of everything."

But only over the airwaves. In Maurice's tactile world, it was almost all ebony—and that's the way Syracuse wanted it. Like many cities across the country, Syracuse accommodated a nexus of laws and informal agreements in real estate, labor, and government that shackled many black people to certain neighborhoods and low-wage jobs. As a result, black families got by on very little income and were jammed into cramped, dilapidated housing owned by white landlords—many of them former residents of the

15th Ward—who lived in the more prosperous
quadrants of the city.[4]

"There was one white family that lived over on
Fayette Street," said Maurice. "But Washington
Street, I don't really remember any white people at
all. There was a bar across the street, he was black.
There was a barber shop, Smitty's, he was black.
There was a big church, Reverend Murphy's church.
He was black. There was Ben's Kitchen, which was
black-owned. You could go in there and get soul
food. There was another bar right down from there:
they called it the 'bucket of blood.' They had a lot of
migrant workers. They'd come here to pick beans
and stuff. Then on the weekend, they'd get it on.
There would be some fighting and cutting and all
that kind of stuff. There was somebody always getting killed there."

Plenty of cash changed hands at the nickel-and-
dime shops that black people owned in the Hostons'
neighborhood, but the real money flowed straight
out of the 15th Ward. Black rent and bank deposits
went to the white captains of commerce, and the
neighborhood's major employers—the L.C. Smith

---

4. These noxious forms of discrimination stunted economic and social growth and explain, in part, the high rates
of poverty that continue to plague black neighborhoods in
the city.

and Corona Typewriter Company and the Continental Can Company—refused black applications.

In the mornings, many black men filtered out of the community for unskilled jobs while women, like Willa, took in washing and cleaned the homes of white families. Ted—who never worked in the factories—moved on from his clerical work to become a maintenance man before landing a bartending job in the mid-1950s at Schrafft's on Warren Street, the first of that storied candy store chain to serve food. "As a kid, looking back, we did all right," concluded Maurice. "I had clothes and plenty to eat and a clean place to stay and sleep. It was good."

Today, the shops and homes that Maurice knew as a child are but visions in his mind. Beginning in the late 1950s, his whole neighborhood was shaved from the earth thanks to a grand urban renewal scheme funded by the federal government. In Syracuse (and across America), slums disappeared, sending some former residents to public housing, while municipal buildings made of poured concrete popped up in the skyline next to Interstate 81, an automobile-age wonder that ran high through the 15th Ward on a 1.4-mile viaduct.

Fifteenth-Ward families without means moved to new housing developments on the East Side, and those who could take care of themselves set down stakes on the South Side, which would become the new heart of black life in the city. Black merchants could have moved to a special segregated business district carved out by city officials, but they chose to follow their customers, who now lived in their own segregated districts. Sadly, the disruption ended up snuffing out a lot of black commerce in the city.

Make no mistake: many black residents celebrated their new apartments away from blight of the 15th Ward. But others chafed. Protesters from local black churches, civil rights groups, Syracuse University, and labor unions marched on demolition zones, picketed construction sites, and organized community discussions, objecting to the dismantling of community and other issues such as housing discrimination and bias in hiring. Nonetheless, the forces of change rolled on. "Black people were together [in the 15th Ward]," said a rueful former resident. "People stayed put. We lost the closeness. The community was great and it's gone."[5]

    5. Dick Case, *Remembering Syracuse* (Charleston, SC: The History Press, 2009), 118.

2

✧ ✧ ✧

REIMAGINING
A CITY

As populations boom in cities such as San Francisco, Boston, and Washington, DC, promising good jobs and exhilarating cultural life, the city located about 250 miles northwest of New York City sits on the sidelines, desperately clinging to its middle class as its net population dwindles. Although population decline in Syracuse has slowed since the peak years of rust-belt erosion in the 1970s, 1980s, and 1990s, when tens of thousands of people disappeared per decade, the city still lost 2 percent of its population between 2000 and 2017. That may not sound like much, but in a city of about 143,000 it can be a fault line that swallows neighborhood schools, shops, and churches. Too often the city must shrug helplessly in the face of those who contemplate leaving: the young college graduate who can't find a job in his field of study, the worker who can't grow in her job because her employer freezes wages and operating budgets, and, worst of all, the chronically unemployed man or underemployed woman who just doesn't care anymore.

But three men in tweed jackets recently claimed to have a solution to the problem. They appeared on a sharp winter's night in 2016 at a seniors center in the northern suburb of Cicero to pitch a grand scheme that promised to stop population leakage. As citizens hustled inside from the blustery weather to hear the story, the trio tugged at their shirt cuffs, standing under glittery shamrocks that dangled from the ceiling in anticipation of St. Patrick's Day.

The three men wasted no time explaining themselves: by creating efficiencies across the region, like sharing municipal services, such as water and road maintenance, and folding city and county governments into one administration, the region might again see job growth, the bubbling spring of new population, and a revitalized urban core.

It was the kind of thinking that had been long absent in Syracuse. Other counties across the nation already provided most services, including education, to their towns and villages, while Nashville, Louisville, Indianapolis, and other cities had years before merged with their county governments. However, such talk rattled many suburbanites around Syracuse, who feared losing municipal jobs, autonomy and, most of all, control over their local schools, although the plan didn't address education. The men in tweed represented the Consensus Commission, an initiative of local business and community leaders. This evening, they were led by co-chair Cornelius B. Murphy Jr., a widely admired Syracusan. Better known as Neil, he used to be the president of a local engineering firm. Then he took over the presidency of the State University of New York's College of Environmental Science and Forestry (SUNY-ESF), growing enrollment and the endowment during his tenure. Quickly making friends with his wry smile and humble entreaties, Murphy once hosted a somewhat imperial fellow college president and his staff in his conference room and, before starting the meeting, circled the table handing out pencils and pads, a task that his secretary in the next room could have easily handled. The visiting underlings were bewildered; they could not fathom such humility in their own president.

On that frigid night in Cicero, Murphy joked about the weather, but the audience stared back at him. The talk of consolidation had well preceded his visit, and the chilled people were having none of it. So Murphy grimaced while he and his colleagues talked up Indianapolis and Nashville, urging the people to imagine one executive, one legislative body, one fire department, one police department. Onondaga County's towns and villages, they said, should merge its fifty-four fire departments, fourteen police departments, road maintenance, and zoning boards. Cost savings, more regional autonomy, and job growth would follow.

A man grunted in the back. To Murphy's side, a fellow Consensus member furiously texted, his hands visible beneath the unskirted table where he sat. The former college president continued: there's the relationship with the state and federal government to consider, he argued. As a larger municipality, the region would have greater lobbying power in Albany and more access to federal dollars. "This can work," he pleaded, approaching his conclusion. "We have consolidated our 911 call center, recycling, libraries, and other services. It can go further."

When Murphy turned to questions and answers, the man who had grunted targeted one of the elephants in the room: the City of Syracuse. He, along with others, feared having to subsidize the wasted city. "Syracuse is a shell of its former self," he growled. "We've already given it a lot of help. It needs to take care of itself." A man in a burgundy shirt added that the city will just gobble up more public dough, inflating his tax bill.

Representing additional concerns, the owner of an ambulance company feared losing his business if emergency services across the county merged, and an older couple argued that money spent on the Consensus work should be used instead to fix Syracuse's aged pipes, referring to the well-publicized spate of water main breaks plaguing the city that winter. Another charged that no city or county leaders could be trusted because they spent money imperiously, like on a new amphitheater on Onondaga Lake that was built with next to no public input. A woman named Sarah threw consolidation advocate Andrew Cuomo into the boiling pot, arguing that the New York governor, by funding local pet projects with state dollars, was dictating the region's future from his throne two hundred miles away.

With that, Murphy flinched. "He can be a bit of a bully," he admitted. "We're not going to kowtow to him."

By then, the advertised listening session had deteriorated into one big anti-government rant, the first local rumblings of the Donald Trump movement. Many people seemed determined to nail Murphy and his colleagues for the sins of a dozen Syracuse mayors and city council members. A woman with unkempt hair who would become a noisy fixture at future public sessions stepped forward from the unruly delegation. People will lose their jobs and their voice, she said, clutching a large bottle of orange soda.

When a nervous yet resolute man condemned the proposal, Murphy appealed to his better side: 77 percent of Onondaga County residents leave their towns to work in another town, he pointed out; doesn't that show a web of interdependence that could be strengthened?

Hewing to Murphy's appeal, a man admitted that the city has to be saved because it provides jobs and recreation and is handicapped by so much tax-exempt property owned by colleges, churches, and other non-profits. The region can only gain from a healthy Syracuse, he added.

"How will this be decided?" called out another voice. By a popular vote, said one of Murphy's colleagues, if it ever makes it to the ballot.

SUNY-ESF's twelve-acre campus, where Murphy still teaches as an emeritus professor, is wedged between the Syracuse University campus and the sprawling Oakwood Cemetery, where many of the city's founding mothers and fathers are buried. A quiet slice of Syracuse, the campus boasts an impressive student center inspired by an Adirondack lodge—replete with a display of preserved wildlife and a vegetated roof. Thousands of students have passed through its halls on their way to jobs in national forests, engineering firms, and urban farms.

A native of Vermont, Murphy arrived in Syracuse in the 1960s to study toward a graduate degree in chemistry at Syracuse University. When he finished, a post-doctorate position awaited him in London, but his wife was pregnant, and they were reluctant to travel. So he took a job at a small engineering company and typed article after article reporting the findings of his work on water management, such as developing filtration systems for sewage overflow.

Despite his transformative work at SUNY-ESF, Murphy's deepest impression on Syracuse may be his work on the cleanup of Onondaga Lake, whose shores the city shares with the suburban town of Liverpool. When white people arrived in great numbers in the eighteenth century and began harvesting salt from the springs near the lake, the big crystal pool was a jewel of the Onondaga Nation of the Iroquois Confederacy, which claimed (and still claims) the land where Syracuse would grow up.[1] As development expanded in the eighteenth and nineteenth centuries and the native peoples saw their land taken from them, hotels and amusement parks crowded around Onondaga Lake. People swam, fished, and boated. But industrialization spoiled the

---

1. The city of Syracuse was incorporated in 1848.

lake. Manufacturers pumped pesticides, heavy metals, and other pollutants into the formerly pristine waters, while the people of the city contributed a steady flow of raw sewage.

By the early 1900s, the resorts were disappearing and, over time, ice harvesting, swimming, and fishing were banned. Regulators and environmentalists deemed it one of the dirtiest lakes in the world and few in Syracuse would disagree: parents warned their children away from the gooey shorelines, while drivers passing by held their noses. With the late 1960s and early 1970s came a national awareness of environmental issues, which locally set off a grand convention of finger pointing. Who was to blame and who would pay for the cleanup? The state sued the county. The county implicated industry. The state sued Allied Signal, whose ancestor companies had dumped tons of mercury into the lake. Then the federal government entered the fray, and the lake became a Superfund site in 1994.

About the time fishing was banned in the early 1970s, Murphy began studying levels of contamination in the lake, and, as his career prospered, a growing movement addressed the cleanup. Honeywell, which had absorbed Allied Signal, finally committed to the cleanup, investing millions of dollars in cash and human resources while partnering with county, state, and federal agencies. SUNY-ESF bolstered the movement, too, with continued scientific research. By 2017, this team of institutions had capped the contaminated bed of the lake, restored some habitat, and promoted recreation on and around the lake.

There remains much room for improvement—nobody recommends eating much fish from the lake, and the smell around certain pockets of the shoreline still offends—but Murphy delighted in the lesson of cooperation among formerly warring factions, so much so that he penned an op-ed in the local newspaper with subtle hints for critics of Consensus. "We're a community struggling to find basically what we want to be in the future," he said later. "We struggled with Onondaga Lake to decide what we wanted it to be and how we were going to get there. If we solved that issue, we should be able to solve the next issue."

Murphy will joke that he should have disappeared from the city the moment he retired from college administration, but he'll add that guilt nags him. Indeed, he said, the region has let down its young people, who must leave in search of stable careers, but it has also failed the impoverished population, who now make up 33 percent of the city, an astonishing statistic.

"I have a summer home in Skaneateles, 15 miles from the city, one of the most gorgeous places on the face of the earth," he explained. "A lot of times when I make that trip out of the city to the lake house, I feel damn guilty. You know why? Because you can see some minority youth who only know ten city blocks and a convenience store. I drive by that corner and I'm not doing anything about it. I think I have a responsibility to do something about it. The other day I was on that route to get out to the camp, and I was at the intersection at South Salina and Brighton. There was an African American woman who had a grocery cart and there were returnable bottles in plastic bags in it. On top of it was a two-year-old and a four-year-old. It was just starting to rain. In my head, I was saying, 'I should pull over. I have a pickup. Throw the stuff in the back of the pickup and drive her wherever she wants to go.' And I didn't do it. There was always an excuse."

It's no wonder that citizens like those who showed up to see Murphy at the seniors center in the suburbs wrinkle their brows when big ideas come their way. Most of the big ideas seem to come from New York state governors, most recently Andrew Cuomo, who has haphazardly showered tens of millions of dollars on Syracuse and the region, inviting corruption among some developers and sparking building projects that fail to reflect the needs or wishes of local people. So the area gets an amphitheater, a film production house that sits empty, and money for hotel refurbishments that the people never asked for. In recent years, it has narrowly avoided an extravagant, Cuomo-supported gondola near the state fairgrounds and a new football stadium for Syracuse University, which, with a one-billion-dollar-plus endowment, doesn't need state aid to stage its gridiron matches.

Because state money had helped fund the Consensus Commission and the governor had threatened to withhold half a million dollars in aid to Syracuse if consolidation didn't take root in the region, people saw Murphy and company's movement as just another careless exercise of state influence.

In Murphy's office, amid tubes and filters that are part of his work on creating small, almost personal, water filtration systems for people in developing countries, he acknowledged the Cuomo problem. "The Governor desperately wants to have Syracuse further along [in a consolidation process] than any other city and county in the state. He desperately wants Syracuse to be a model. But [his threat to pull aid] was not constructive to this effort, and it leads to people thinking, 'This is driven by the governor or this is driven by the county executive, and we don't trust them.'"

Indeed, the Consensus work had become so much more politicized than the grumbling at suburban meetings might suggest, intensified by a fierce grudge between the governor and Syracuse Mayor Stephanie Miner, a couple in dire need of relationship counseling. When Cuomo came to power in 2011, they seemed to be happy Democratic partners, but two years later Miner criticized the governor's economic support of cities and quickly found herself on the curb. He removed her from state Democratic party leadership and made County Executive Joanie Mahoney, a Republican, his main regional contact.

All of a sudden, Miner, who many thought had a future in statewide politics, was a lone wolf, alienated even from her city council after a dust-up involving members' access to city computers. Many read her every action, including her increasing absence at Consensus meetings, where she was ex-officio, as a protest against Cuomo or Mahoney. Despite taking principled stands against the sweetheart deal to fund the football stadium for Syracuse University as well as the reckless distribution of tax breaks to developers by the county, she was still often seen as a malcontent who put up walls around the city.

Miner's unpredictable performances on Syracuse's political stage also carried over into the city's Skiddy Park troubles when, two weeks after the riot, she clutched the edges of a podium set down in the middle of the now-silent battlefield and called for unity in addressing inequality in Syracuse. Strangely, she avoided specific reference to the Father's Day incident, the police, or the shooters, reciting instead the Prayer of St. Francis in one of the least Catholic neighborhoods in the city. She launched into a history lesson on red-lining, which denied many black Syracusans federally guaranteed home mortgages starting in the 1930s, but she failed to link such real injustices to the collapse of reason a fortnight before.

Instead, Miner ceded pointed commentary to her fellow speakers on the dais. "It is sad to hear how our community [members] kill each other slowly," said a representative of the Spanish Action League. "The war will continue unless we bring peace among each other and forgive each other. It is our decision to help and be helped."[2]

Around the city, irate voices rang out on the Skiddy Park controversy. The local newspaper editorialized against the District Attorney Fitzpatrick for stalling the release of information related to Officer Francemone's shooting of Gary Porter, while the police union president, fearing that Francemone

2. Chris Baker, "Mayor Miner Delivers Sermon on Poverty and Racism on Near West Side," updated July 1, 2016, http://www.syracuse.com/news/index.ssf/2016/06/mayor_miner_delivers_sermon_on_poverty_and_racism_on_near_west_side.html.

might be a target in the DA's probe, defended her. Meanwhile, Black Lives Matter demanded that the state take over the DA's investigation. "The officers who help determine what 'officially' happened that day are the same people who deprive black people of their rights," the group charged.[3] As officer-involved shootings seized the headlines in Oklahoma, Louisiana, Illinois, California, North Carolina, and elsewhere, the Justice Department dispatched a lawyer to Syracuse to calm police–community relations, but local waters neared the boiling point, particularly among those who believed Francemone had shot Porter without justification.

3. Patrick Lohmann, "Black Lives Matter: State Should Have Taken over Syracuse Father's Day Shooting Probe," posted August 23, 2016, http://www.syracuse.com/crime/index.ssf/2016/08/black_lives_matter_state_should_have_taken_over_syracuse_fathers_day_shooting_pr.html.

3

✧ ✧ ✧

COMING TO
SYRACUSE

When Ted and Willa Hoston's older children reached
their teens in the 1950s and 1960s, nobody talked
much about police–community bonds. It was a one-
way relationship: you dealt with the authorities on
their terms, not yours. Yet their son Maurice Hoston never clashed with the police, and when he ven-
tured out of his neighborhood, his interactions with
whites rarely alarmed him. "Mom would always get
us dressed up to go downtown. We'd go there especially on Saturday and see the cartoon shows and
serials before they showed the regular movie. That
was the best times. They had a movie theater, we
used to call it the Nob. That's where we'd go a lot
of times on Saturday morning because they were

cheap. You could pay a quarter or something and get in. That was some good times. As far as that goes, it wasn't that we had to sit in the balcony and the whites sit down there. Never any of that. I'd seen the movie *Blackboard Jungle* when I was fourteen. They start playing 'Rock Around the Clock' and, boy, we jumped up in the aisle and got to dancing. Black and white. It really began to rock and roll . . . people were being people. It was a good deal."

It was only as he entered a Catholic middle school—St. John's on the North Side—that he noted the line between him and the majority race and began to understand the racial violence and intolerance writ large in society.

"Back then you didn't go to the North Side after dark," he said.

That was mostly an Italian-American area of town. You wouldn't go up to [the Irish neighborhood] Tipperary Hill. Stay the hell away from there, too, because you weren't welcome. When I started going to St. John's, it was all white except for four blacks. Myself, a girl named Kay-Kay, and then two brothers, the Johnson brothers. Both of them were really good basketball players. There was never any out-loud racism at St. John's. I can't remember anybody calling me a 'nigger' or anything like that, but there was one incident: I was in class and my favorite nun teacher, I think they were trying to collect money for something, said, 'Come on now, let's not be *niggardly* about this.' Of course everybody in the class gasped . . . I just had to play it off. Like, 'Well, I know what it means.' But it was just an incident. One time I was laughing and joking with a guy and I said, 'Well maybe I'll have to dance a jig or something like that.' I was thinking like Irish jigs or dancing. He said, 'Do you know what you just called yourself?' I said no. I'd never heard 'jig' used in that way. It was just . . . things would come up.

Of course, most of the kids at St. John's, their fathers had office jobs and were very upper middle class, had a lot of money. I remember going to some of their homes on James Street. Back then they were fabulous places. A bunch of us were standing around one day and somebody says, 'Hey Mo, what does your dad do?' I said, 'Oh he works for Schrafft's restaurant. He works on the bar down there.' They went, 'Your dad's a lawyer? I didn't know that, man. You're a rich bitch.' I didn't tell them any different. I was bothered because I should have straightened them out instead of being ashamed about what my dad did. But I think about that. I was just trying to belong.

One of the first times I really felt mad about the way I was being treated was when my friend and I got hold of the *Jet* magazine and it showed Emmet Till in there. Where they had beat him and hung him just for whistling at a white woman. That made us angry. Angry and hurt and confused.

With the destruction of the 15th Ward, Ted and Willa moved to public housing on Westmoreland Street on the East Side that sat on a crest looking over toward the drumlins of the North Side. It was a step up, as far as they were concerned. Their apartment was sturdily constructed and provided more space for their growing family, not to mention household appliances and a neighborhood quieter than the one they'd just left behind. "It was mixed," added Maurice. "And everybody seemed to get along pretty good. Most of the kids I played with were white kids."

Maurice's enlistment in the army in 1959 coincided with the budding of his parents' professional success. They both had taken up janitorial work, and, in time, would own their own cleaning service. "My dad was always working on the weekends," said Rob Hoston, Maurice's half-brother and the second son from Ted and Willa's marriage. "When we were old enough we'd go with him. I had one job with him, sweeping up the front of Lincoln Bank, which was on the corner of Cherry Street, near Genesee Street. I made ten dollars or something like that. He was always working and doing things like that. Later on in his years, he got into carpet cleaning."

As the civil rights movement gathered steam across the country, exposing legal discrimination and racial atrocities, the Hostons seemed to embody an alternate narrative of the black experience. Ted and Willa were thriving economically and their public housing seemed to model a bright future for the races. "We had friends from all walks of life, this is back in the late fifties, early sixties," says Rob. "We had a lot of good friends, a lot of good times, a lot of kids. We all played together. All the parents knew each other that lived in the apartment buildings. People would have parties in their apartments and my parents would go. It was really good, and I remember thinking when I got in junior high and high school—it was the time when a lot of racial tensions were going on—that none of that was back on Westmoreland Street. There were black kids, white kids, Native Americans. We just all played together. We were all friends. None of that stuff ever presented itself. If it did, I don't remember it."

While the 1960s raced on and letters from Maurice arrived from army bases all over the world, Rob took up the bass and older brother Ken the electric guitar. Together, they joined a racially integrated band that played all over Syracuse and in the county. When people walked in a club and saw the band for the first time, they assumed it was either soul or rock, but the salt-and-pepper congregation played everything from Wilson Pickett to the Rolling Stones. "From what I recall, somebody only

shouted something once," recalled Rob, avoiding
specific mention of the epithet. "There weren't so
many black rhythm guitar players like Ken standing
up there playing Beatles stuff. It would kind of throw
people a little, and he did it really good. I guess
we educated a few people back then. We were just
guys out there playing, and we were happy going
into clubs and parties and frat houses. They just
loved the band."

Then on a day that seemed like every other day,
the din of cars and trucks on the new Interstate
81 and bulldozers taking down the last of the 15th
Ward in the background, Rob discovered that the
racial terrorism of the 1960s had finally come to
Syracuse. "One night," he offered,

my brother, myself, and some of the guys in the
band and a couple other friends were going to
May Memorial Church on Genesee Street to hear
a band, so we went into the place and there was
a fraternity there from Central Tech High School,
which was downtown at the time. My brother
and I were the only black guys in the group and
they wanted to beat us up, kill us. They had their
knives out. There were five of us and twenty of
them. They were calling us all names. That was
pretty scary, until the minister came out and got
in the middle of the things. We backed out and
drove to this club called Wanda's because one of

my friends knew some people who were down there from our high school, which was Nottingham. So we told them what happened and they actually got in cars and went out and found these guys from Central Tech. When they came back, they said, "We took care of them for you. You're not going to have anybody bothering you." And these were all white guys.

These were tense times. I was in the cafeteria once, and a racially motivated fight broke out. Some of the white kids would go to the other schools and start stuff and that's what happened that particular day. They happened to pick on some of the black athletes, which was kind of a mistake. It was an awful thing to see. The principal ended up getting hit in the head with a chair. It was one of the worst things I'd ever seen along those lines.

Rob Hoston had lived blissfully unaware of Syracuse's racial turmoil, then nearly a decade old by the time he witnessed the cafeteria fight. In the early 1960s, black people had protested against urban renewal's decimation of the 15th Ward, and, then, with the help of national leaders from the Congress of Racial Equality (CORE), demonstrated against the local power company's whites-mostly hiring practices. In the wake of riots in nearby Rochester in 1964, black leaders warned that racial violence could also come to Syracuse, which proved prophetic. Although Rochester's maelstrom was far more destructive and deadly, black groups rampaged in and around downtown Syracuse in 1967, foreshadowing three nights of violence the following year that were marked by four firebombings. Throughout those troubled times, voices from the black neighborhoods blamed the violence on the police's heavy-handed targeting of black people and the discrimination that they met in every quarter of Syracuse life. A black clergyman complained to a newspaper reporter, "When the police normally see three or four black kids on the street, they shout, 'Niggers, go home.' And riding around . . . with their shotguns sticking out the car window—they're always more concerned with putting down the violence than with getting rid of the causes—too often they are themselves the causes."[1]

As Rob Hoston observed, the violence moved into the schools in the fall of 1968, forcing the temporary closure of three of the city's schools after several fistfights and incidents of rock throwing. A white student was arrested after school authorities discovered three bottles of gasoline in his locker.

And the conflict raged on. In 1970, near the scene of 1960s protests around the destruction of the 15th

---

1. Thomas A. Johnson, "Syracuse Unrest is Laid to Police," *New York Times*, Sept. 12, 1968.

Ward, rocks, bottles, and sticks flew through clouds of tear gas as black students clashed with city police over institutional discrimination in Syracuse University's football program. Violence bled into the following year as six young black males who walked into a white neighborhood on a dare were set upon by police, sparking three days of armed conflict in the nearby black neighborhood. Blacks lobbed twelve Molotov cocktails at passing traffic, one of which badly burned a white motorist, followed by showers of rocks launched by youngsters who told reporters that they were just lashing out at whites who attacked them. In response, whites threatened to form vigilante groups and shoot any threatening person who approached them. A national reporter in town to cover the conflict learned about other heated exchanges from a black developer who had recently proposed building a housing tract on the fringes of a white neighborhood. "We met with whites in the Valley Presbyterian Church to ask their cooperation," said the man. "And they told us, 'If you build it we will burn it down.' The police had to come and escort us out of it; the whites were just that hostile."[2]

Could this be the city that harbored runaway slaves in the nineteenth century? It felt more like Birmingham of the 1960s.

2. Thomas A. Johnson, "Syracuse Split by Racial Views," *New York Times*, August 11, 1971.

While Rob Hoston tasted racial violence for the first time, Elise Baker from Mississippi settled into the city's South Side, where many poor blacks had settled. She had arrived in Syracuse at the tail end of the Great Migration, which had brought hundreds of thousands of black Southerners to Northern cities starting in the 1920s. Her parents, though, had come before her, leaving the infant Elise with her godmother.

Recollections of Mississippi, though blurry, dwell on fishing with a cane pole and choruses of "We Shall Overcome" in her church. She recalls images of a murdered black man in the woods but can't be sure what she saw. Her parents retrieved her when she turned six, and the Syracuse sun shone warm on her skin, as it had for the young Hostons. Everything seemed possible.

"Our community was beautiful," she recalled.

You didn't throw trash in the yard, and at that time it was black and whites in the community together. Next door we had an old man named Snoop. My mother couldn't afford to send me to camp. But Snoop paid for me to go to camp. So we had a lot of help in our community whether you were black or white. The whites that stayed in the community were people that were able to deal with blacks and know how to manage together. Most of it was about keeping your community clean, going to school. I was like tops in spelling bees. I was a person who excelled a lot in education. I don't know where I get it from, but it was there.

My mom was afforded to buy a house through a program that helped blacks. I remember how proud she was and that was right directly on the South Side. Our streets were beautiful. There were plants. We took pride in gardening and putting grass in our yard. None of the houses was like they are now. The roads were nice, the houses were all painted and the flowers were planted and trees. We had something to look forward to each day after school. We would play games, hopscotch and all that stuff. Then we'd climb cherry trees and pick berries. It was good. It was community cohesion. We had a good childhood as far as that.

We had corner stores owned by blacks. We had a lot of things with people just working. Especially in the nursing field for the women. Some men, they were working for the railway, jobs that probably they don't want to work. We had community stores: Frank the pizza man; Lamar Lee, which was a business owner; Loblaws, which was a grocery store. We had credit, and come pay it off at the end of the month. That old-time stuff.

We had welfare with the government cheese and the turkey and the Spam and all that stuff. That's how they did welfare at that time. They came and checked on you. They sent case workers out. Made sure the house was up to par. Made sure that there was food. Not like now where they give them PA [public assistance], send them some money on a benefit card and what they do is spend it on drugs and stuff. Those people back then couldn't have spent it on drugs because it was for food and rent.

There were still black families who cared for their properties and their community and learned how to live together. Peace and love. It was a lot of that. And you didn't even see the police that much. Very seldom. We had the bowling alley. We had places to go. We had things to do. We had teen centers that we could go to in the evening. We had the churches. St. Anthony's had after-school programs. We had all kinds of things that made the community what it was. It wasn't about money, and you didn't have the gun violence.

Baker grew into a woman who's her own statement: subject and verb. Pro-black, pro-community, pro-hope, Baker prays twenty-five of every twenty-four hours in the day and trains a laser eye on young people who scatter up and down the streets of the city. On the sidewalk in front of her downtown floral shop, she recently spied a young immigrant, probably a refugee, clutching papers and scanning the storefronts looking for the US Citizenship and Immigration offices. She charged into the sunlight, clutched the man's arm and gently led him to the right place, this while calling across the street to tell a young construction worker she knew to put on his dust mask.

She's been a wife, a mother to foster children and her natural children, a counselor, a concert promoter, and an activist. Everybody knows her face if not her name, and she knows theirs. In the 1980s, she worked as a secretary and then hopped over to the massive General Electric plant. When GE folded in Syracuse, she followed her job to Poughkeepsie, but she soon returned, hiring on with the Syracuse City School District, where she mentored troubled kids, including a rapscallion named Stefon Greene, although she wasn't certain Stefon was so troubled.

The years she has spent guiding kids from the deteriorating streets of Syracuse have radicalized her. She will slap down any hand that imperils her community, as many times as it returns.

You're not gonna come in front of me and sell no guns. You're not gonna come in front of me and sell no drugs. That's what I'm talking about. I don't want to live next to nobody that's selling drugs because I tell everything. I tell, and I don't tell just to be snitching. I tell because I want to make a difference. I want to save a life. I want to keep the community better if I can. If not, then we got to fight about it. I don't want that. There's too many kids dying by the wayside. Everybody says, "Oh them kids, you can't say nothing to them." Yeah, you can. It's how you say it. You can't cuss them out and then try to chastise them because if you do that, you gonna bring out the worst of what they got in them already.

In the wake of the Skiddy Park violence, it was clear that the national epidemic of police shootings of black suspects, broadcast via social media and amplified in the mainstream media, had altered the conversation and merely confirmed what Elise and her former charge Stefon had known all the time: that police gunfire must be second guessed.

Stefon elaborated:

Does Syracuse have racist police on the force? Yes. An officer worked at my high school for a long time. I've seen him get in fist fights with students. I've seen him take girls and slam them on the table and I've seen him mace multiple students in the hallway to break up a fight, mirrored by my mother saying, "I know him from the streets. He's racist." Syracuse hasn't had a police shooting of a black man in this post–Trayvon Martin world, post–social-media visibility, that's what makes Skiddy Park unusual. Has Syracuse had parties like Skiddy Park before? Yes. Have things happened there before where gun shots were fired? Yes. Those things have happened. But have police ever shot anybody? No. That's what makes it unusual. Have cell phones ever been so relevant in terms of seeing all this evidence and all these things that happened? No. And that's the difference. The big difference is exposure and the culture.

Echoing Stefon's observations around the interplay of race, police and media, Elise accused the local television news of indicting Gary Porter, whom she knew, before anybody determined whether or not he had fired a gun or if Officer Francemone had justifiably shot at him. "I've had the opportunity to know him from his heart," she said.

I do know in life that he's made some mistakes. We all have. But because the media tried to portray him as a villain, I did not like it. I think they should research things a little bit more before they tag people. Our city tags these kids with a lot of stuff.

Television viewers just see what they see: a lot of blacks and the people at [Skiddy Park], which is the small screen of things. I sit in the house and I watched it over and over again, and I'm looking at the missing pieces, saying what happened here and why was this? Why did she shoot into the crowd of people? Why? There has to be an answer. He got shot in the back. How did he get shot in the back if he was doing something in front?

Why was she shooting? Why in the initial video were [the people who swarmed around her] saying, "Give me your badge, give me your badge?" Why were they attacking her? They would only attack her if she was doing something to the crowd. But that's my opinion. I could be wrong. But those are the questions that I would need answered in order to understand it. I don't think he was trying to shoot her. I don't believe that because I know the individual. Unless he was defending his life.

In early August of 2016, Onondaga County District Attorney Fitzpatrick determined that Francemone had justifiably fired her gun at Porter, that when he turned to his side there was ample reason to believe he was making moves to fire at her. After all, he'd been firing his gun up to the point Francemone shot at him and had ignored her demand to drop his weapon. Authorities found that Porter's blood alcohol level was 50 percent over the legal limit and that he had marijuana in his system.

At the press conference to announce that he would not be charging Francemone, the DA praised her decision to forge into the crowd to find the other men who were firing off shots: "It's one of the bravest things I've ever seen in forty years."

But the story was far from over. Hours of disturbing video had emerged from security cameras and social media accounts, showing four men firing shots and others trying to stir up anti-police fury as officers tried to secure the crime scene. The local newspaper rounded out the picture: "After the shooting, a crowd attacked police officers with bottles, rocks, trash and part of a bicycle and a female sergeant was also attacked and bitten."[3] None of the four shooters were ever identified, but twelve males and one female were recognized from social media and surveillance video and charged with rioting and other crimes such as drug possession, trespassing, and resisting arrest. By the end of the year, seven had pleaded guilty and received short prison sentences. Six others opted to fight the charges. A January 2017 trial would determine their fate.

3. Charley Hannagan, "Judge Sentences Father's Day Rioter to 3 Years, Denies Attempt to Withdraw Plea," accessed September 28, 2016, http://www.syracuse.com/crime/index.ssf/2016/09/judge_sentences_fathers_day_rioter_to_3_years_denies_attempt_to_withdraw_plea.html

4

✧ ✧ ✧

REFUGE IN
THE CITY

Every year after the college graduation season, Syracuse families tally the missing, their sons and daughters who come home for a few weeks after commencement and then pack their bags for Boston, Washington, New York, Charlotte, where jobs and better weather await. There's the political science major who just left to run a political campaign in Los Angeles, and his sister who relocated to Brooklyn, where she teaches elementary school students, and the law school graduate who grew up down the street whose parents wept when he chose to raise his family in Chicago, and his friend who applies his engineering degree in the suburbs of Washington, DC. How do you quantify the loss of so many who could focus their energy, training, and knowledge on the Syracuse region's questions? Even those who never went to college consider life and work beyond Onondaga County. Yes, many people will choose to stay, but the tide of young blood rushes toward the open sea.

But sometimes new people wash up on the shores of Syracuse and bring with them creativity and vigor. It could be a husband or a wife who arrives with a native-born spouse who misses home too much to stay in Atlanta or Philadelphia. Or a fresh face drawn to an institution of higher learning or one of the city's few thriving corporations.

In 2006, a native of Portland, Oregon, sailed into Syracuse to take up graduate studies in landscape architecture at SUNY-ESF, Neil Murphy's university. After receiving her master's degree in 2009, Jessi Lyons and her husband moved into a house on Midland Avenue on the South Side and, not long after, she gave birth to twins. Since her husband was still working on his doctorate at Cornell University, about an hour's drive from Syracuse, they might have picked up and moved to Ithaca but the cost of living there is high and, besides, Jessi had become a player in local urban agriculture. Before graduating, she had co-founded Syracuse Grows, which fosters a network of neighborhood farms and gardens throughout the city, all in service of cultivating community and promoting locally sourced food. Around that time, a few people with Syracuse's Brady Faith Center, a Catholic social services ministry, were thinking about urban farming in a big way and reached out to Jessi. She didn't blink. The product of a vegetarian home, she brought an unquenchable passion for small-scale farming. "I grew up eating out of the garden and valuing eating out of the garden and gardening with my father. My very first place out of college I worked on a farm and I helped run their market garden. Then at my apartment we put in a garden. I need to be able to grow."

She also brought to Syracuse a vision of urban rebirth. She had watched Portland, with its reputation for gloomy days and blighted neighborhoods, become the hipster capital of the world, with a vibrant downtown, buoyant economy, and forward-thinking public transportation strategies. Make no mistake, the Rose City was no Eden—soaring real estate prices ostracized the middle class, homelessness pervaded the city, and the Trail Blazers often played some of the worst basketball in America—but Syracuse stood to borrow a few pages from the playbook of its western sister.

When spring came in 2016, she and a small team carved out the Brady Faith Center's six-acre plot in the heart of the South Side, the first steps in a restless vision that included goats, poultry, nut trees, and mushrooms.

But Jessi soon learned that Syracuse had its own playbook. As anxious as she was to begin work on the farm, lawyers told her that the city's zoning board would never grant a variance to cultivate the land, despite positives vibes that were coming from Mayor Miner's administration. The property, formerly home to a drug-ridden apartment building, was zoned residential and seemed likely to remain that way.

She'd already confronted more than a few challenges. Some of the land on which the old apartment complex sat was contaminated, which forced her to create a meandering crop pattern, and neighbors around her had complained about losing the field where their dogs shat. Still others thought that an urban plot in a black neighborhood somehow smacked of sharecropping in the old South. But she told anybody who would listen that she planned to plow ahead with or without the variance. And that she did. By early June, a week before the scheduled board meeting, she had already planted rows of tomatoes and had begun to lay drip line alongside them.

The board meeting just days away, a dirt biker tore across the cultivated field and over the drip line. Then a neighbor corralled her, ranting that a ballfield on the lot was better than a farm. "He just keeps at it and keeps yelling at me," said Jessi. "As he goes to leave, it just hit me like a brick that I had forgotten to note in the zoning application that there's absolutely no way that the lot could be used again for housing; it couldn't be successfully sold as a residential property. But the other permitted uses included community centers, recreation fields, churches and schools. That complete narrative was missing from my application. And here's this guy who's like, 'It should be a ball field.' So he doesn't know that he was really helping me because then I realized, 'Oh my God, I dropped the ball so badly.' So I spent Thursday morning documenting that there were already plenty of ballfields in the area."

Jessi walked into the zoning meeting with her Brady Faith team along with a teenager named Jaelle who had worked with her at Syracuse Grows. "Everything at a zoning hearing feels hostile," she recounted. "Like the person before us: she had a multifamily home that she just wanted to zone the right way as multifamily because it had never been zoned that way. And they just were coming up with an excuse to make it difficult. There was nothing negative about what she was saying. But it was almost like they had to make it seem like they were putting her through the wringer."

Jaelle stepped up and made a plea for the farm using notes on his cell phone, and the air lightened. The board members smiled, and Jessi thought about her ballfield inquisitor who had unwittingly improved her application.

"I was told it was a three-week process before we hear anything. So we all go out, take pictures. I was like, 'Yay! We got it over with. That's great.' So it was just a really feel-good kind of thing, beautiful day. I walk down the street to my car and I see the Director of Planning and I was like, 'I just had my hearing.' He was like, 'I know. It was great. I was in the back. Why aren't you sticking around for the decision?' I'm like, 'Huh?' So we got back there as they were finishing up the last hearing. Within two minutes they decided on ours, and it was unanimous, and the chairman winks at me and says, 'Can't wait to see how it works, guys. Good luck.' So that was pretty great."

By embracing the Brady Farm, Syracuse recalled its deep history in agriculture. Of course, in the nineteenth century, the city served as a port for regional farms that shipped their harvests to markets via the Erie Canal, and much of the city itself was agricultural in its early days. Even into the mid-twentieth century, farmers still cultivated slivers of land along the southwest side, and area gardeners have never stopped entering their wares in competition at the New York State Fair in late summer. Beginning in the 1800s, the Syracuse Chilled Plow Company and other manufacturers in the city supplied farm implements to the nation, and in the midst of a statewide decline in farming during the early 1900s, the Syracuse Chamber of Commerce, cognizant of its reliance on the farming economy, organized a statewide convention to discuss reversing the trend. Later in the century, Carrier Corporation manufactured huge refrigerators for farm use, and General Electric experimented with large-scale hydroponic farming, raising tomatoes, lettuce, cucumbers, and other produce in the middle of Syracuse's frigid winters for shipment to grocery stores and restaurants.

The arrival of Jessi Lyons and other urban farmers was merely the beginning of another chapter in the city's long agronomic history.

One of the first signs of life on the Brady Farm was a long row of okra.

The brains in New York agriculture proclaimed that okra would never grow upstate. The plant needs a longer growing season, not the three or four months that the Syracuse climate stingily gives backyard planters and high-acreage farmers.

The vegetable likes long, hot summers and won't object to dry stretches. In the early going, a languid white flower appears on the sturdy plant and then gives way to a fibrous pod that must be plucked when it reaches the size of a roll of quarters lest it become too woody to eat. Okra lovers slather it in cornmeal and deep-fry it, toss it sliced into soups and stews, or brown it in their iron skillets.

Slaves from Africa brought the plant to the Americas starting in the sixteenth century and by the eighteenth century it was a staple crop across the South, that home to sweltering summers. Even Thomas Jefferson raised it at Monticello.

Nobody knows exactly when okra came to the garden plots of Syracuse. But it probably arrived with poor whites and blacks who journeyed north during the great migration of the twentieth century. They cultivated it in their backyards next to corn, tomatoes, cabbage, and green beans. Sometime in her ten years here, Jessi Lyons learned about their little okra secret.

By late August, the Brady Farm had become a forest of vegetables. Sunflowers stretched to the heavens, corn stood like tall soldiers in formation, and cucumber vines crawled across the field. Jessi and her six employees and numerous volunteers sold the harvest at local markets while neighbors who had routinely scowled at them in the spring now waved and shouted hello when they passed.

The change in mood among the neighbors first drifted back to her when she asked a group of youth volunteers from the suburban town of Baldwinsville to go door-to-door in the neighborhood with letters inviting residents to pick the black raspberries in the wooded areas of the farm and visit one of their three market stands around the city. Residents whom the young people met praised the farm and asked thoughtful questions.

Over the students' week of volunteering, they quipped that they had tired of waving at the neighbors and hearing shouted encouragement from passersby. Said Jessi, "Their reflection was, 'We're really missing out. We think we have it so good where we live, but the reality there isn't that overwhelming kindness and community spirit and support and people really rallying around something.' And they hadn't really recognized that. They had their preconceived notions about the South Side."

The greening of each furrow brought more encouraging news: a new county grant came through to help with distribution; more stands appeared on street corners and at farmers markets; use of a city-owned greenhouse for winter planting was offered. Newspaper articles celebrated the young people in the neighborhood who volunteered or got part-time jobs on the urban farm as well as the insoluble vision of its down-to-earth manager.[1]

1. Jackie Warren-Moore, "A Garden of Eden Blossoms on Syracuse's South Side," accessed September 16, 2016, http://www.syracuse.com/opinion/index.ssf/2016/09/a_garden_of_eden_blossoms_on_syracuses_south_side_jackie_warren_moore.html.

But the okra plants were the biggest reward in Jessi's eyes. She noted the hardening of their sturdy trunks and the dark green leaves that you might imagine wrapped around the battlements of a medieval castle. In the mornings, Jessi's fingers slipped past the branches' tiny thorns and cradled the plant's dazzling blossoms before turning to the pods that had grown to three inches and clipping them for market.

Once she had gone on vacation and returned home to find her workers waiting to harvest the okra at twelve inches on the advice of a customer, a black female. Jessi shuddered, knowing that the price of length is taste and tenderness. The worker protested that she would always take the advice of a southern black woman over Jessi's on the subject of okra. "Well," countered Jessi, "I've had plenty of southern black women give me their two cents about how to grow okra. So don't do it again." A brief firestorm flared up as aging southerners turned up their noses at the abnormally long vegetables. "Then I get these phone calls, and I have one woman leave me a three-minute-long message, chewing me out over the okra. Then another guy called and said, 'You let it get big. It was pretty good, but I had pieces in there that weren't tender. Next time I come, I want four pounds but it can't be bigger.'"

This was actually conversation in controversy's mask, just what Jessi wanted. People in nearby homes were talking about the farm and this vegetable that connected them to their traditions and their southern roots. Drivers recognized the plants and slammed on their brakes to advise workers on how best to harvest the pods. "Don't miss them. The branches hide the treasure." They remarked on the freshness of Jessi's bounty compared to the brownish okra they found in grocery stores that shipped it up from Florida and Georgia.

A thrilling dynamic somehow formed on the South Side of Syracuse: people reconnecting with an edible remnant of their heritage, daughters and sons passing on advice from their migrant parents and grandparents, varied races and cultures coming together, the land reverting to its original purpose.

Jessi said she would make the labor-intensive okra a you-pick crop next year, at one dollar a pound, half price. "There's only a few things that I'm willing to let people pick by themselves. But this is one of those things that I could triple what we grow easily and let them do that. And let them be obsessive about it like I am. But I'm obsessive because they're obsessive."

In a city coping with population decline, Jessi's arrival in Syracuse from Portland and her choice to hang on signaled hope. On the opposite side of the city there were more like her, people who had traveled from faraway places, such as Haiti, Eritrea, Afghanistan, Iraq, Kurdistan, Sudan, and Bosnia. A man named Justo Hector Triana had fled the island nation of Cuba in 2014.

On a September afternoon, he walked the north shore of Onondaga Lake, where he can view Syracuse's modest skyline, missing his wife and worrying about his daughter and, particularly, his son, who would soon turn fifteen and have questions about girls, school, and the future.

He could have predicted such feelings on the day he walked over the US-Mexican border and surrendered himself as a refugee to the American authorities. Forever, he had chafed under Cuban thought police, watching his tongue on political questions, seeing professors hauled off to prison for protesting the government, living in poverty as a child when the Soviet Union's collapse spelled the end of direct aid.

A trained lawyer and classical guitarist, he had been ordered by Raúl Castro's government to serve a new hitch in the armed services. It would have been his second, the first served when he was in his late teens. But with so many young men fleeing the country, the military was replenishing its ranks with veterans.

"They only wanted me to be there a couple of weeks, for drills," explained Justo. "They are like the North Koreans, doing these drills all the time, every two years or six months, it depends on how the political atmosphere is. I had paid my tribute to the army." In September of 2012, he reported for processing, but when an officer called his name, he refused to step forward. She raged at him, threatening jail time and demanding that he state his opposition in writing.

About one in ten recruits refuses to enlist, estimated Justo, and most are left alone. But he figured that his status as a professor doomed him. "Once you make a move, and you let them know what your feelings are then you are in trouble," he said. "You wouldn't have a stable position anymore. You would always be the black sheep. It's not safe anymore." Military officials followed up with regular visits to his home, just to remind him.

And then his suspicions came true. The government slashed his hours at the university. Saying nothing to colleagues and friends, only to his wife and children, he plotted his flight, promising to arrange the family's passage once he settled in the United States.

Fortunately, America's Cuba-friendly "wet-foot, dry-foot" policy was still in force; he needed only to show up at a land border. Cubans attempting to arrive by boat were generally sent back. So, in August of 2014, he flew to Mexico City and caught another plane to the border city of Reynosa, where he presented himself to border agents.

After a short time in Miami, the US Office of Refugee Resettlement moved him to Syracuse, where he was given housing and a stipend, the cost of which he would have to repay in six months. Immediately, he began the process of bringing his wife and children to the United States under the Cuban Family Reunification Program. It would cost him $2,000 to bring his wife and $2,000 for each of his children.

He soon learned that Syracuse was home to many of his fellow citizens. A Cuban man rented him a basement apartment at a reasonable rate, and like many other doctors, lawyers, and engineers in the refugee community he took a job well below his qualifications on the nighttime cleaning crew at Upstate University Hospital, where other Cubans worked.

In the day, he searched for more challenging work. A job interview in the department of foreign languages at Syracuse University soured when a professor learned that Justo despised the Cuban regime. "The woman who interviewed me had a Che Guevara portrait behind her desk," he recalled. "He was looking at me behind her, and at the very moment I said that I was a Cuban refugee I was done. I have a master's in Latin American Culture, almost a PhD. By my heart I can recite from many Spanish poets. I know Latin American literature, poetry. I'm a native speaker, you know what I mean? And I didn't even get an email after that. And I'm not a Republican." He was luckier with the Syracuse City School District, which hired him to teach English to Spanish-speaking children. Soon after, the Northside Learning Center, a literacy organization, asked him to teach adult refugees. Occasionally, he picked up a few bucks playing his guitar in churches and at dinners around the city that showcased food cooked by refugees.

"I'm surrounded by immigrants all the time," he said.

> Mostly Cubans, Puerto Ricans, and Mexicans in the mornings, and Russians, Sri Lankans, Burundians in the evening. They are salt of the earth people. They are so naïve. You have to get to know them in order to love them. It is hard because most American people don't interact with these guys. Most of them are very hard workers and nice people and we really enjoy the company with each other.

> I like this multi-culturalism. These people speaking tons of languages, especially the ones from Africa, they speak one language with four

dialects. A man from Burundi probably speaks
three or four languages and speaks French. But I
love it. I can try to learn some Arabic. I feel pretty
comfortable with that.

Many refugees from Africa are very hardworking people, just like Americans. They are
very honest, very respectful. But they lack the
literacy. They lack the basics. That's sad. The refugees who come from Europe . . . they are very
hard working, too. They are more literate. Most
of them are professionals. They have their engineering degrees, medical degrees. Ones from the
Middle East are very smart. They know things.
They, too, have their degrees.

In the late summer of 2016, two years after Justo came
to America, Donald J. Trump rolled to the Republican nomination for president on an anti-immigrant
wagon. Ultimately, Justo expected Hillary Clinton to
win the office but lightly conceded that he could live
with Trump if need be. "I came to this country. I
was nobody when I came here. I'm still nobody. But
I value democracy. If 51 percent of Americans decide to be anti-immigrant, I will get around that. I
didn't have the guts to speak up to my dictatorial
government, so I won't do it here. I have to be fair.
I don't like many things, but I'm not even a citizen.
I will accept whoever America chooses as a president. If there are anti-immigrant people sometimes

it's because immigrants have their responsibility for that. I would like to work on that side . . . let the people I interact with get to know me and let them know not everything coming from outside of the country is bad or is something that has to be feared."

In Justo's mind, the promises of opportunity in America are as much his as anybody's, and he planned to restart his academic career by applying to PhD programs at Syracuse and Cornell. Inspired by the immigration stories all around him, he set his sights on cultural anthropology, hoping to write a dissertation on ways in which immigration influences religious beliefs.

"Some people who are not religious by nature when they experience a really serious trauma in their lives, like migration, they stick to religion or become more religious," said Justo. "And usually religion goes with the people. And religion changes as a result. For example, when the Africans were taken from Africa to Cuba, they brought their gods and they found a way of camouflaging their gods behind Catholicism, so in the end they were praying to a white god which in reality was an African deity. Migration changes things. For example, some Muslim women in my class, according to their religion, they are not allowed to shake hands with men, but they've been forced to soften that strict interpretation here in order to get a better job or to get along with people in a better way."

Back at the Brady Farm, the flourishing okra and a column of sunflowers had walled off the eastern side of the acreage, blocking the view of cyclists, pedestrians, and cars that raced down the street. You could be crouched down behind the barricade weeding or picking vegetables and never see a soul passing by. In late August, Jessi pulled her Volkswagen to the side of the road near the imposing sunflowers, hopped from the car, and disappeared behind the okra plants. She was inspecting her watermelon patch when she looked through the plants and locked eyes with a boy riding a bicycle with his friend. It seemed odd because usually kids on their bikes paid little attention to the workers. But she quickly forgot about it and refocused on the crops. Then a strange noise disrupted her work. She slipped back through the okra plants, and saw her car door hanging open. The boys had gotten away with her purse.

A few days later, they returned, telling the workers that Jessi—who wasn't around that day—had promised them a job. The workers moved the boys along. But one of the kids reappeared a short time later and approached Cheri, one of the employees, who by then was the only worker there; the others had gone to lunch. The boy started up again about a job, while his friend stole away into the supply shed and filched pruning shears, a clippers, and Cheri's purse.

But just like in the comic books criminals still return to the scene of the crime. When Jessi arrived back at the farm, the boys cycled up to the okra.

"I had my eye on them," said Jessi, "and one of them comes around and says, 'Hey I got to talk to you.'" With that, she snapped a picture of him.

"Did you take a picture of me?" he growled.

She said, "I did because you guys stole my purse and my friend's purse."

"That wasn't me," he replied, coolly.

"Yeah, it was."

"How could you know? You couldn't have even seen us."

"You're talking yourself into a hole, buddy."

In the corner of her eye, she saw the other teenager, approaching in his maroon high-school football jersey. She pivoted toward him and snapped another shot. "And he says, 'Did you just take a picture?' And I said, 'Yeah, I did. I want my stuff back. You stole from us.' And then he started calling me racist slurs and awful obscenities. He said, 'I got a gun. I'm going to fuckin' shoot you, bitch. I'm gonna show you what I fuckin' got.' He starts digging into his backpack, so I'm calling the police. I get on the phone, and he packs up and they bike off."

The police arrived in an instant, but the boys were quicker. They disappeared into the maze of streets surrounding the farm.

Later in the afternoon, a few people who worked for the Brady Faith Center recognized the boys in Jessi's pictures, but they hesitated to tell the police. The director proposed calling their families. Jessi said, "I am supportive of that because the last thing I want is another kid in the justice system . . . but to have threatened somebody with physical harm like that, that's a game changer."

She fretted over how much to tell her husband, who sometimes worried about living in the city. But her blues over the loss of safety on the farm weighed most upon her. "This really bums me out because 99 percent of our interactions are neutral to overwhelmingly positive and it takes these two guys and now everybody's scared. I can't have people there alone. I'm there by myself all the time, and now I can't be there alone. That's a major problem. If they were just thieves that wouldn't scare me as much, but he was really very aggressive and threatening."

Before the thefts, she had thought okra might be an ideal trademark for the farm. That didn't change. Its bloom communicated hope, but the plant's thorns added another layer of meaning now that the teenage boys had pedaled into her life.

5

✧ ✧ ✧

NO PLACE
MORE VITAL

Thorny, too, had been the fortunes of Syracuse University basketball. The 2015–16 program had weathered coach Jim Boeheim's six-game suspension early in the season for numerous violations of NCAA rules that happened on his watch, and fans had winced at the smug analysis of talking heads in sports media who just knew the team would implode by mid-winter.

But the players had shrugged off their misfortunes, not to mention Boeheim's demoralizing and public rants against his players—he had notably called one of his heart forwards a "last resort" player—to slip into the NCAA tournament. Valiantly, the team disposed of Dayton, Middle Tennessee State, and then Gonzaga in a breathtaking 63–60 victory that led to the so-called Elite Eight and an Easter Sunday match-up with the well-oiled University of Virginia squad. Whoever won would compete in the national semifinals.

Across Syracuse, religious obligations and holiday dinners gave way to sheer anticipation of the Orange's resurrection. Families clutching their small children and bowls of Buffalo-wing dip shuffled across the street to watch the game with neighbors while men and women gave their dogs a quick walk before settling in to absorb the action. On University Hill, the orange lights that ringed the Carrier Dome, where the team plays its home games, blinked to life and cast a glow that blended into the evening sky.

S. Salina Street, the main artery through the South Side, emptied out like an old Western town before a gunfight. Men slipped inside after one last smoke, and children still searching for an undiscovered Easter egg turned toward home.

Monday morning would be so much brighter—at work, at school, on the corner—if the team lived to fight another day.

Of course, few in the basketball world expected Syracuse to mount much of a challenge, despite its marvelous string of victories. The Cavaliers just outclassed the Orange on so many levels. Their players were cool and consistent, their coach composed and gentlemanly. And, true to predictions, on that

Easter Sunday in the tournament city of Chicago, Virginia dashed into the lead early in the first half and refused to let go. Until late in the second half. A young player named Malachi Richardson, who in a strange ritual after hitting a basket circled his eyes with his thumb and index finger as if to form glasses, launched a humbling streak of three-pointers. And then the Orange rolled out its fearsome full-court press and shut down the Cavalier offense. Embodying the come-from-behind spirit that is the city's eternal if somewhat thinning fuel, Syracuse walked away with a magical victory. And the families with their dip, the dog owners, the smokers, and the Easter egg hunters leapt in jubilation. For a moment, being in Syracuse was like riding an electrical current. There was no place more vital. Monday would be great.

But for another shooting on the West Side of Syracuse. While the Orange wrapped up their victory on television, nine shots rang out in the real world near Skiddy Park. One bullet hit a ten-year-old child in the ankle, and another killed a thirty-five-year-old man named Francisco Tejeda. A black sedan sped away toward S. Geddes Street.[1]

1. The Tejeda killing remains unsolved.

While Syracuse celebrated and the Tejeda family mourned, Elise Baker fretted. She and her son, Brandon, hustled to put together their 315 Spring Dance Fest, a variety show for youth in the city. Many days, Brandon slipped out of the floral shop to sell tickets during high-school lunch periods while Elise lined up security services and searched for sponsors to supplement the funding should ticket sales flounder. "I'm moving and jiving and shucking all the time," she said. With the show just three weeks away, no sponsors had stepped forward and ticket sales were slack. When asked, Brandon was too embarrassed to say how many tickets he'd sold.

Elise first promoted shows in the 1980s when she brought to town soul stars like Blue Magic and Harold Melvin and the Blues Notes. Since then she had sponsored gospel concerts and tried her luck promoting tours, all with little payoff. "I've taken shows as far away as Mississippi and they've crashed. I didn't even have money to get home. That's how bad they crashed. I went to Carolina one time. Crashed. But the show that made me stop was a white comedian I took to northern New York. We were in the car riding back, and I remember he said to me, 'Elise . . . what is your purpose for doing these events? Your purpose should be to make money.' I said, 'I do want to make money but that's not my main purpose.' He said,

'Are you kidding me?' He said, 'You done lost your mind.' They started to feel sorry for me because they see me lose so much money. They said, 'You must be crazy as H-E-L-L.' What they said that day hit me like a light bulb and something went off in my head, and it shut me down. I said, 'They right.'"

She turned to more reliable pursuits such as her school district jobs mentoring students and raising foster children, a total of thirty-three over the years. In short, children became her thing.

"We should be soul watchers to our children," she implored.

You not going to let your children continue to do wrong if you can teach them right, will you?

Good parenting don't stop because they become eighteen. It don't stop because you let them talk back to you. If you let your children talk back to you and say words to you that you know that they should not do then that's your fault. It ain't theirs. It's your fault because you are their parent. They are your child. I don't care what nobody says, I will slap mine in the mouth if he's a young person who decided that he's going to do that. Send me to jail then. It will be well worth going. But I bet you he will never do it again.

At fifteen, I did something and my mom told me to get out. The tone was set from the beginning. My mom also worked on putting fear in me.

My mother didn't stand for a lot of things from us, and one thing we didn't do was challenge her. If we did something, my mother didn't spare the rod. We knew not to do certain things. But we got something different. My mother was there, she was working, and she was trying to make a difference in our lives. When she wasn't there, somebody was there to take care of us.

Back in the days, we had wholesomeness. A woman was taught to get married. We had that picket-fence syndrome. Two children or four, a boy and a girl, a little white house, and a picket fence. We were taught this stuff. Today, you get your sneakers, you go and get your hair weave. You get what I'm saying? It's a different image. You get the booty injections, the breast injections to look like Kim Kardashian or Beyoncé. You get gang violence or rap or play football. These are the images that are being taught to our children.

You see them little girls walking down the street with their children and they on the cell phone. The cell phone is so big that they forget that they have their children with them. One morning there was a girl downtown and she had a little baby about three years old with her. She was on her cell phone and she wasn't paying attention to her child. I said, "Baby, you gonna lose her. Somebody can get her," and she got so mad at me. I said to her, "I'm only telling you out of love."

She said, "It's my child. I can do what I want." I said, "You're right. It's your child. But the point is this, she can dash out in the street or somebody can come behind her and take her."

We should all take our part and fix some of the problems. We could fix some of them. We may not be able to get them all. But we can fix enough to make a difference. That's all it's about.

By mid-April, memories of Syracuse basketball's glories had dimmed. After beating Virginia, the team fell to North Carolina in the Final Four and the city refocused on immediate concerns, which for Elise and Brandon Baker meant staging the Dance Fest. Early in the morning, Elise had driven to New Jersey to pick up DJ Lilman, the headliner who preached positivity amid the mind-crunching music and beats of his performances. But she refused to bow to the long day. By show time at Henninger High School on the North Side, she had donned teal slip-on shoes and a matching spring jacket. She took the microphone and repeated her mantra, "Everything we do is based on love."

Brandon lingered behind his mom in a denim shirt and candy-apple red hi-tops, his large frame and stacked afro unmistakable in the crowd. Over the speakers, he introduced the talent and thanked

Elise for the inspiration she provided, his voice cracking with emotion.

While a chilly breeze cut across the parking lot outside, Mark Muhammad, a school board member and a minister in the Nation of Islam, looked over the small stream of people entering the building. A woman insisted on entering without paying. Both Elise and Muhammad tried to divert her, but they gave up so as not to be diverted themselves. The sounds boomed from inside the gymnasium.

On the basketball court, three krump dancers stepped out. One with dyed braids and droopy pants took the lead and with his partner acted out street-life disruption: drug dealing and violence set to rhythms that burst from the speakers like machine gunfire. A third dancer joined the hard-life ballet, surging forward and receding with her troupe. The performance never sugar coated. It was like the country blues of Elise's home state of Mississippi, which starkly painted the grisly back-alley knife fights and carnal temptations, lessons in the cold, hard facts of the streets.

Another dance collective emerged, black-power emblems on their T-shirts. Erect. Proud. While they jerked and thrusted, a cell phone flew from one dancer's pocket. Across town in social halls and studios, perhaps at that very moment, freckled girls who are Irish dancers fluttered in the air while other children tap-danced at recitals. Here, routines seemingly inspired by Beyoncé's pole dancing or the booty battles in a Nicki Minaj video fanned out across the floor, a thundering contrast in this city of contrasts.

The evening surged when the emcee invited children under eight to compete in a dance contest. Shuffling and gyrating like modern Solid Gold dancers, two of them rose to the top, earning a few bills from their judge's roll of cash. The smaller kids among them waded out into the crowd, nudged by their mothers, and incredibly they popped up unscathed from time to time, bobbing like sea hawks in the churning surf. A man wearing an anti-gun-violence placard snapped selfies while a group of city girls called the Dancing Diamonds waited for the chaos to subside so they, too, could perform.

Then DJ Lilman bounded to the front of the arena, but he failed to churn the crowd as Syracuse's home-grown children had. He led the kids in dance routines and doled out dollar bills to students who recited their times tables—all very positive in contrast to the suggestive sock hop of a few minutes before but, ultimately, kind of bland.

The next day, no reviews of DJ Lilman's show or the little dancers appeared in the news media because local reporters don't concern themselves with the city's subterranean. As a consequence, few Syracusans knew anything about this youthful explosion in the young black community that had rolled out free of gunfire and knife fights. Dozens of images bounced around the Facebook echo chamber where friends and friends of friends could see, but as far as the city at large was concerned Elise and Brandon Baker's North Side party was a secret meeting.

A few weeks later, Elise gingerly settled into a chair at the central library on Salina Street, just a few doors down from her flower shop. Since the Dance Fest, she had taken a fall and weathered a cancer scare, but she had remained on alert, catching up with the flock who clamber down Salina each day and cooking up plans for a breast cancer awareness event in the fall. To find her quarry, she must keep moving, she said. "It's either that or lay down and die or let something take control of me. I'm not ready yet. I got to push 'cause I got to do some things."

Rubbing her forehead, she bemoaned the losses she took on the Dance Fest. She had given away too many tickets and sponsors had never materialized. A donation from the Job Corps as well as some food sales had rescued her. But don't talk about the lady who had tried to enter for free. "My son asked me to deal with her because she refused to pay. And Minister Muhammad also went to her. So several people went to her in regards to that and she refused.

Because of the stress that I was under and what I knew what would take place if I allowed myself to get caught up in it, I backed off. I just stopped and prayed. I said, 'God, if you don't come in, then something is going to change.' . . . I've seen her since then. Wrong place, though. Because it was in church. So I didn't confront her. But rest assured as I am sitting here at this table, I am going to confront her."

Begrudgingly, she acknowledged the good in the evening. "It was successful for the purpose and the meaning. Yes, very much successful. The children enjoyed themselves. They got a chance to display their talents, and I hope that love was projected enough for them to understand that they're greater than all the stuff that's happening out here in the community. And that they can go places without having all these confrontations. But if I would have acted on that woman, it would have come out different. And I knew that. I knew it was a setup from Satan, in other words."

Back on the larger stage, Neil Murphy's consolidation movement had encountered roiling waters. A chorus of dissenters routinely attacked the plan in newspaper editorials and at community meetings, and certain politicians began to show their fear of being consolidated right out of a job.

The Republican chairman of the county legislature lumbered up to a downtown microphone and
pronounced that there would be no vote in his body
to allow a referendum on the subject. To make matters worse, the county comptroller shredded consolidation's core selling point—cost savings—credibly
proposing that the region could save bundles more
by battling high state taxes and the surging cost of
Medicaid, 25 percent of which must be covered by
New York counties. Others turned up their noses at
any cooperation with the city, like the anonymous
blogger "No More Mr. Nice Guy": "Merging would
then turn the county into one big city of Syracuse.
They will then have the ability to move people
around the county for such things as schooling and
housing. Shipping city kids to other schools and putting shelters in your neighborhoods, because when
we merge we become one big, happy family. Right."

Grumbling assaulted the commission members
from below and above. Fortunately, the two most
prominent local politicians had agreed to withhold
their opinions until Consensus issued its final report. Until they decided not to.

In a major speech, County Executive Joanie Mahoney lambasted critics of consolidation, as most
expected she would since she'd been a champion of
the movement from the time it first emerged. But
the poison bomb dropped a few weeks later when
Mayor Miner charged in a speech to a conservative

group that the preliminary Consensus proposal lacked sufficient detail. And even more damaging was her promotion of the oft-mentioned belief that the plan was nothing more than the county trying to take over the city, suggesting to people of color in the city that, in effect, the white county was out to gobble them up.

Miner's remarks winged Consensus, and Murphy fumed.

"We asked all the local politicians, 'Please do not weigh in on this until the public comment period is over,'" he complained.

> "Let the public put on the table what their concerns are. We'll give you a summary of that, unfiltered, you'll get that, but please give them their due to weigh in before this is politicized." The county executive in her state-of-the-county speech discussed Consensus in four pages of her text. That was not constructive to this effort.
>
> I can't tell [whether Miner's comments] have to do with her relationship with the county executive which is, at best, weak today. Eighteen months ago they were close to being on the same page relative to modernization of government. Today they seem to be much further apart. I've asked the mayor on two separate occasions, "If a metropolitan government, from your perspective, wouldn't work, what would work? Where can we

go in this to make a difference in a way that you
could feel more comfortable with?"

In his office, Murphy went quiet. Evidently, the
mayor had withheld comment.

The retired university president dwelled for a
moment on his youngest daughter, who had just left
Syracuse for Atlanta with her husband and three
children. His wife cries in their absence while Murphy looks to Consensus to bring them back. He returned to his message:

> I think there's a reasonably conservative streak in
> people in Central New York. There tends to be an
> inertia against change. At the same time, you've
> got young people who are looking for something
> different. You have parents that have children who
> are making decisions about what they're going to
> do and why they're going to do it. I think there's
> an interest on the part of those two segments
> of the community to do something different to
> make sure their children and the young people
> who want to stay here have a successful career.
> It's kind of the yin and the yang of it.
>
> Why do we have two economic development
> agencies that are at odds with one another?
> Shouldn't we have only one? Shouldn't that be
> solely focused on doing whatever it can to get
> the best business opportunities in Onondaga

County? You have towns competing with other towns for a hotel. Or a box store. I think if we're all pulling together, we have the opportunity to make this a better place.

Relative to the concerns of the city about losing its voice, we've actually found that the voice of minority people has increased in those areas [that have seen consolidations]. In other words, prior to metropolitan government being adopted, the minority participation in city government in terms of common councilors and that kind of thing was about nine percent . . . single digits . . . and in each one of those cases it doubled following developing a metropolitan model of government. Some of them have gone the route of special districts in order to make that happen, but it's been an objective and that is one of the objectives here, that those from diverse backgrounds can't lose their voice.

I remember one presentation that I made in the city where there were probably three people who were very vocal. There was one individual who stayed in the background and would shout things out. There were a number of difficult questions and probably 90 percent of the way through a young man stood up and was literally lecturing everybody that was there, like 125 people. He said, "You better pay attention to what's in this report because there's some really good things.

You better pay attention if you want your sons
and daughters to stay in Central New York. If you
want your grandchildren to stay in New York."
And then he sat down. And I had the mic in my
hand and I put the mic down. I walked down to
him, and I gave him a hug. That's when I learned
that he was an alum of ESF . . . And he was an
African American. I said, "You have to understand, the student is still teaching the teacher."
But that young man . . . you could just tell from
the passion in his voice, his aspirations were in
this community. He just wanted to have something he could grab on to.

6

✦ ✦ ✦

BARRIERS EVERYWHERE

The notion of grabbing onto something, clinging to a hope or a vision of a better day, fueled Ted and Willa Hoston's migration to Syracuse in the 1940s and sustained their lives through the passing decades as they edged into the city's middle class. They established their own cleaning business and Ted picked up golf. But the crowning symbol of the family's ascent was a new house on Northway Street on the East Side of Syracuse near Le Moyne College. "They were proud to be able to get that house, get out of public housing," said their son Rob.

That was a huge thrill for them. They almost couldn't believe it, but they worked hard to get to that point. Late nights, a lot of weekends. My dad was always working on the weekends.

They were just great to have around, very supportive of anything that we did. When we started to do the music thing, they were a little apprehensive. . . . "I hope you're not going to do this all of your life." My father was really funny about it: When we got old enough and we were doing weekend things at the frat houses, he'd say, "You're going to have to start paying rent. You're living here, eating here, you can contribute." My mom was great. She was very calm, really very easy going. As we got our own lives, they were proud of their sons [Maurice and James] coming home in uniform.[1] Very supportive. They would come out and see us play. My mother would say, "I don't know where you got that from." When we were just kids growing up, she'd be doing dishes and she'd sing. When I look back on it, my mother could sing. She'd sing all these Dinah Washington songs. Maybe that's where we got it from.

But Ted and Willa were also watching two branches splinter from their tree. Maurice, who had left town

---

1. James was Willa's son who was adopted by another family. However, he eventually followed Willa and Ted to Syracuse. After his military service, he joined the Syracuse Police Department.

to join the Navy in the late 1950s, was struggling with alcoholism and drug abuse, and, in Syracuse, their only daughter Debra was about to choose the dangerous South Side streets over upward mobility. Debra Hoston, who would become Stefon Greene's mother, was eleven when her parents and siblings moved to Northway, but while her brothers Rob and Ken stuck with the books and sharpened their musical chops, she dropped out of high school, searching always for the next party. "I had good morals and values, but I started hanging out with the wrong people and started going to parties," explained Debra. "Back then, you went to house parties down in the basement, dancing. And that's where I met Stefon's father. And he was from down on the South Side and that was it. I started hanging out down there. It was a whole other environment, something I wasn't used to. And I liked it. It was always a bunch of drama and something was always going on. I just really navigated right towards it."

Ted and Willa frowned on Debra's move, knowing that the South Side had deteriorated since the time of Elise Baker's dreamy memories of the neighborhood. By the late 1970s, black residents there, many of whom were falling below the poverty line thanks to widespread job loss in Syracuse, were watching whites evacuating to the suburbs and drug dealers taking over prominent street corners. According to

Debra, there was no question that East Siders shied away from her new stomping grounds.

"The South Side boys back then liked the East Side girls because we were considered good girls," recalled Debra.

> Stefon's father, Glen, went to Central Tech, I went to Nottingham, so a lot of the guys from Central Tech would go up to Nottingham on their lunch breaks and they all had cars and so did Stefon's father. He had a car when he was sixteen. We rode around. We just got together. I got pregnant when I was seventeen or eighteen. That's when I had my oldest son. My mother and father were shocked, but they weren't like, "Oh my goodness what are we going to do?" At that time, my grandmother was alive and she was feisty, that was my mother's mother, Helen Henderson. In her eyes, I couldn't do no wrong, none at all, so she was like, "Just leave the girl alone, we just going to have a baby." And that started that. I was nineteen when I moved out and got my first apartment, which was down on the South Side . . . My mother helped us and Glen's mother helped us and we just did our thing. He always worked and I stayed at home because I never really had a lot of jobs.

Central to Debra's new South Side life were drugs, mostly heroin and cocaine. "I never smoked weed," she said. "I just started with the hard stuff and 'bam.' Crack rocks came out, and I started just like that. People find that so strange that I didn't smoke weed." Her new lifestyle consumed her. "I went two years without seeing my mother. The only time I might go up there is when I wanted something, but when I got really bad off, I didn't go around at all. My mother used to tell me that she'd say a prayer for me at night. She didn't really understand what was going on. My brothers really didn't understand what was going on." When the police arrested her for the first time and a judge sent her to rehab, a useless sentence as it turned out, she finally visited the family house and explained her problems.

"It pained my mom," said brother Rob. "It hurt her a lot. And my father. I think they saw what my sister was getting into, and they saw how she was being hurt. And we did, too. You can talk all you want to her, but she's a Hoston. And there's a stubbornness."

Debra Hoston's stubbornness may have been nothing, though, compared to the rock-hard resistance the Consensus movement confronted in another community forum, this one in Fayetteville, New York, a village near Syracuse with its own board of trustees and local services. In contrast to the grumbling Neil Murphy and his friends had met in the northern suburb of Cicero, resistance to municipal consolidation in high-tax, high-income locales like Fayetteville promised to be fierce.

Fayetteville and its sister village Manlius (which share schools and police) had carved out a bucolic enclave away from the hazards of the city, with public schools among the finest in the state, crime rates fairly low, and town services reliable. There, a homeowner going out of town on vacation can ask the local police to cruise by his house daily while he tans on a Caribbean beach. In return, residents pay a dear price. Property taxes on modest homes reach $10,000 a year and higher.

Wisely, Murphy had stayed home for this Consensus pitch session, handing the rostrum at the local middle school to retired congressman James Walsh, one of the commission's co-chairs. Walsh arrived late on a brisk March evening and waited for local politicians to greet the assembled and introduce him. Although shades of the former politician remained in view, Walsh surprised the assembly with his candor, admitting that during his thirty-two years in Congress he "never moved the needle" in Syracuse, despite bringing millions of federal tax dollars back to town. He repeated the litany of local problems—job stagnation, population decline, urban decay, inefficiency—as he diverged from

Murphy's main argument, which had pressed cost savings as consolidation's big payoff.

Instead, he pleaded on behalf of Syracuse, acknowledging that many in the county would rather not subsidize the city. "This is not about cutting property taxes," he argued. "It's about recognizing the importance of the city. You can't have suburbs around an empty core. We've got to help it through a difficult time."

The citizenry hungered to reply, but not to disagree with Walsh, at least initially. The first audience members to speak up blamed the region's woes on larger forces, such as Obamacare, rising taxes, intrusive mandates, soaring labor costs, and Governor Andrew Cuomo, who, they argued, used state tax dollars to dictate to local communities. Walsh concurred: "He should run Albany and let us run Onondaga County."

Then the compass ticked slightly to the right. Faintly echoing nativist sentiments expressed during Europe's recent refugee crisis, other attendees championed the local identity of Fayetteville and Manlius. "Services and money should stay in the community," uttered a local man, igniting an anti-city powder keg.

In another man's mind, the city's crumbling parking garages symbolized its corruption. (Few would disagree that many of the garages appear to

have been relocated piece by piece from the abandoned Chernobyl nuclear power plant site.) That set
off a woman seated next to him who decried the
weedy entrances to the city, trash on the streets
and sidewalks, and the recreational walking path
that hugs Onondaga Creek, which the city, indeed,
could do more to maintain. Somebody sitting next
to her charged that Syracuse is an albatross around
Manlius and, should Consensus pass, the county
would have to bail out the city. Her town would be
dragged down, she predicted, because of decades
of mismanagement in the city.

"Manlius has everything to lose," said another.
"And Syracuse has everything to gain."

A few days later, after Walsh had flown back to
Washington, where he is a registered lobbyist,
Murphy turned to the misconception that under
consolidation the county would have to bail out
the city.

> Well, state law does not allow the city debt to be
> paid by somebody out of Manlius. City debt would
> have to be retired by the residents in the city. It
> would not be able to address financial issues of
> the past. It would be focused on financial issues
> of the future. The other thing is, the city of Buffalo

is the second largest city in New York state, and
they get about $150 million in state AIM funds;
the city of Syracuse gets $76 million.[2] If we had
a metropolitan form of government, metro Syracuse would be the second largest city in New York
State. Presumably, if there is equity, there would
be the additional payments to the Metro government analogous to Buffalo getting $150 million.

The other way is . . . when we look at Louisville
and Indianapolis, and the others that have gone
through this, they've generally had an increase in
economic opportunity. In the end, getting more
economic opportunity would yield more return
that again will address the issues going forward.

I don't completely understand the anger [in
Fayetteville] because 77 percent of the people [in
Onondaga County] that live in one governmental
jurisdiction work in another. So it may well be that
some of the people in Fayetteville are saying that
the city is screwed up, but they're the ones that are
using services in the city. We all know a lot of them
do. Do they not have a degree of responsibility if
they fundamentally are using the services? When
they come in, if the streets aren't plowed, they're
bitching like everybody else. But they'll go to the
Landmark Theatre for a performance. They'll go
to any number of pretty decent restaurants in the

2. AIM stands for Aid and Incentives to Municipalities.

Armory Square area. I'm not suggesting that they would have to assume responsibility. But if they come in to the city to work, should they not pick up some degree of responsibility?

To me, that 77 percent figure is a big deal. It fundamentally means we're all in it together. When you look at poverty among minority groups in the city, I think it takes a pretty callous individual not to say, "Shouldn't we do something about that?" Do we know what to do? I don't think we know yet. But I think we know of some things that can better change that picture.

Perceptions. From the point of view of Fayetteville, the city dangled on the edge of oblivion. However, Murphy saw salvation in governmental reorganization. Others discerned in the nightly scenes of shootings and stabbings across the city a jurisdiction ruled by chaos. Stefon Greene still saw community, even in the wake of Skiddy Park, which many assumed represented the worst kind of urban pathology.

"Black community has grown from hundreds of years of slavery," explained Stefon.

You're talking about black people being segregated in a particular neighborhood. Then you're talking about so many disenfranchised people who come together with their resources so that everybody can be taken care of. In those historical senses, that's where community comes from. Then, in to-day's times, you have a party at Skiddy Park to celebrate things. Everybody knows each other. Because so many people know so many people, it turns into a way bigger thing. I remember my father taking me to multiple barbecues in a day when I was a kid. So he would pick me up on a Sat-urday and we'd go to a thousand and one places. He'd be like, "These are your cousins. Go get your food and play with the kids." It's that community sense that brings people together and it turns into a lot of people really quick. There's always a bar-becue for somebody who's passed away or some-thing like that. I think it's about coming together.

It doesn't happen in some white neighborhoods and suburban neighborhoods because people there still tend to live their own lives. However, my mom is in what is considered a senior building in housing, but they live such a community-oriented life there. She takes multiple ladies to the store there because they don't have cars. She goes and gets money from the ATM for a lot of ladies in her building so they can pay their bills. She be-came the computer person because I showed her all these things about the computer. She opens the computer and pays people's bills online, buys them things online, and all that stuff. So I think that is down to the roots of being community oriented. You do other things for your neighbors and they do things for you.

As far as Skiddy Park, I still walk through there every day. In the morning time, I drop the car off to my mom, and I walk down to work. I'll get off of work and walk down and get the car. Do I know things happen? Yeah. When we lived in Pioneer Homes there were a number of occasions when they were shooting and the bullets were hitting the porch. My older brother lived in the "Bricks" in the Central Village, and one day they were shooting down there and the bullet went right through his front window and it was lodged in his wall. They ended up moving but not for that reason.

Just because I live in this bad neighborhood and I hear all this regular gunfire, doesn't mean I'm OK with it. I think that's where people outside of the culture tend to offend when they don't mean to. At the same time it's like you don't want to look at all the video and all the footage of Syria and all these war torn countries and think, "Oh, well, they're used to getting their homes bombed every single day. They're used to not eating for weeks at a time because they can't get any aid into the country." Nobody would ever say that. But at the same time, people in the urban

communities and the black communities don't
like it. They don't want it to happen.

So why not leave the violence rather than stay in
the community?

Black people's answer—I will unofficially speak
for all black people—has to do with white privilege. I define it as a number of things including
where you come from, what you have, and the
opportunity you have to go other places. So with
white privilege you might come from a good family who have money and they can take care of
you. It's somebody you can call to be like, "I need
this because I can't do this." Your ability to get
something on credit. Financial. To be able to walk
into a bank and be like, "I need a home loan." If
you're going to meet a realtor and you're going to
meet somebody in order to move to a new possible neighborhood for the first time and you're the
black family coming in, no matter how prestigious
you are or how educated you are, you're always
looked at in a different way. So I think it's where
white people don't realize the white privilege that
they have. They can't understand why you just
can't leave.

   But there can be a value in leaving that all behind. The value in it is that you are taking your
own children out of a cycle and you're changing a

cycle that it is super hard to get out of. There's a radio guy I listen to on *The Breakfast Club* in New York City, and he was a DJ for a lot of famous rappers and made a lot of money, invested his money. He always talks about his kids and I follow him on my Instagram. His kids go to nice schools and his son and his daughter are out of this culture that he was so entrenched in and raised in and built his success off of. But they're out of this cycle. I want my children to be as educated as possible, to know all these things. I think it's just about breaking out of the cycle. I was broken out of the cycle, and I'm totally different than how my father is today. Do I know a lot of things about the streets and stuff like that? Yeah, because I spent a lot of time in it. I've done bad things and I'm lucky that I never had a serious enough charge that sent me over the hill. Because when you go to jail then you're in this lifestyle. You're never getting out of it. That's it. I was lucky enough to never spend time in jail and I was lucky enough for an education that clicked for me before I went over the hill. But it didn't take away all my friends and all the people I know that are still entrenched in that culture and that makes me sad. It makes me upset, it makes me guilty. All I can do is hope to bring my children out of the cycle. I don't want my son to live in the 'hood, and I don't want him to see those things. But at the same time I want him to learn those lessons.

The lessons of the city know no limit: overcoming obstacles; resisting temptations; learning to deal with various races and nationalities; developing an authentic sensitivity to ignorance and material need; getting along without the very best. Sons and daughters of Syracuse will grow up with something precious that is elusive in the suburbs, albeit such thinking breeds a certain snobbery among denizens of the rust-belt metropolis, including social service providers, television producers, and this writer.

It has also crept up on Jessi Lyons, like when a group of young people from the western suburbs spent a week with her at the urban farm sowing and hoeing. "They wanted to do other things like serve food and build houses," she recalled. "They didn't like being stuck farming." The kids complained, and their parents complained. But Jessi shrugged. "You know what? The heart is open to what it's open to and not everybody's heart is open to the same stuff, so too bad they didn't get something out of it. They wanted to be served a particular thing in their service."

She may have reached her limit some months later when an email arrived from a student who attended a parochial school located outside the city. The young scholar had researched urban farming and wished to share her findings with the Brady

Farm. Whatever the student's intent, Jessi bristled, sensing a condescending tone. Biting her tongue, she invited the teen to be part of a larger discussion of farming that might include her research. "She's just a high-school student, so I didn't want to be a jerk, but I did need her to recognize the appropriateness of her suggesting that she has something to teach us urban people. You want to encourage that interaction between suburban and urban, but a lot of the tension is over that whole savior mentality, 'Here is how I'm going to save you.'"

7

✧ ✧ ✧

WELCOME
TO AMERICA

On the North Side of Syracuse in 2016 a smiling old man from Sudan limped down the sidewalk in front of an Italian bakery that had served up crusty breads since the time when the neighborhood teemed with families newly arrived from Europe. As he made his way along the street, a loyal old Italian woman who left the city for the suburbs years ago shuffled into the store and ordered rolls from an employee who mostly spoke Spanish.

A few blocks away, children who had fled the prospect of slaughter in the Congo tumbled down the stairs of the splintered two-family home they live in on their way to a grocery run by a Bhutanese man. In this part of the city, greasy-spoon diners had become Asian takeaways and former hardware stores now promised an impressive selection of Middle Eastern goods.

Germans dominated this quadrant in the nineteenth century, but by the 1930s Italians ruled. Ostracized by the city's larger Irish population, who lived on the West Side, they established their own grocery stores, taverns, social clubs, bakeries, and churches, and launched their children into Syracuse's rollicking civic and business life, where they would become city council members, priests, and college presidents. But by the 1960s, the call of suburban life had begun to drain the North Side. Businesses failed, population and household income spiraled down, and crime rates soared. By the 1990s, only a few vestiges of the old Italian world remained: Lombardi's Grocery, Our Lady of Pompeii Church, Di Lauro's Bakery. Many alumni of the neighborhood gasped when news came down not long ago that the prominent Sisters of St. Francis convent—occupying eight acres in the heart of the neighborhood—would be sold to a developer who planned to build a residential community called The Kimberly, a name hardly in keeping with the area's ethnic heritage.

In the old days, young people across the neighborhood flocked to the sprawling Catholic Youth Organization (CYO) on N. Salina Street to play basketball in its upstairs gymnasium, dance to records by The

Fifth Dimension, and fill a Saturday afternoon with knitting classes and music lessons. These days, the old building bustles as ever, only now it serves the burgeoning refugee population. New arrivals from the Congo, Myanmar, Bhutan, Pakistan, Sudan, Serbia, and a dozen other countries visit for career counseling, English language lessons, medical check-ups, and help with the serpentine path toward American citizenship. In the early mornings before school, women in hijabs, children clutching school books, and men with worried looks on their faces line the hallways. Around every corner, there's a staffer or an immigrant rushing along. During school hours, the chaos subsides, but by mid-afternoon, business at the Northside CYO cranks up again as students, workers, and wanderers flood back into the building for the services provided by the local chapter of Catholic Charities.

By the time the new wave of refugees began arriving in big numbers, the city had established a mechanism to greet and resettle them. Two social service agencies with funding from the federal government handle most refugees, taking care of rent, healthcare, and other basic needs while helping them find jobs so they can begin to repay the $2,000 loan from the US Office of Refugee Resettlement.

Churches, synagogues, and mosques pitch in to help while the Syracuse City School District and other organizations teach English to adults and children and provide job placement. After five years, refugees may apply for naturalized citizenship.

Since 2000, more than 10,000 refugees have come to the city, flooding desolate neighborhoods mostly on the North Side and taking menial jobs and opening businesses. A handful of these men and women find work with the very same social service agencies that held their hands when they arrived. And some leave town. According to an estimate by a local employment consultant—himself a refugee who works closely with new immigrants—about 5 percent move on to other states, following jobs, family, and warmer weather.

To be sure, the arrival of refugees has highlighted the city's compassionate side. Mayor Miner made accommodating refugees one of the hallmarks of her administration. Smiling case workers wait at the airport for newly processed immigrants while students from Le Moyne College and Syracuse University structure class projects around the new residents. Churches adopt refugee families, local high schools stage cultural nights that spotlight the traditions of the new students, and legions of workers from social service agencies work on a daily basis to make the refugees' transition successful and welcoming. A local entrepreneur named Adam

Sudmann has partnered with the local community college to open a restaurant featuring international dishes prepared by refugees, and he organizes quarterly dinners in community halls to celebrate the culinary magic of other new arrivals.

But refugees can also find Syracuse spiteful. Crime that has plagued the North Side for years makes no exceptions for newcomers, and one immigrant from Bosnia, in an interview, told of a police officer who stalked her, pulling her over regularly as she drove at night between her waitressing job and home. Anti-immigrant protests have cropped up from time to time, and people from Bhutan, Somalia, Myanmar, and other nations have described brutal assaults and cruel slurs by homegrown Americans and by fellow refugees who harbor grudges from the old countries.

However, few would go back to the war, corruption, and repression that plague their native states, as Justo Triana attested to, even as the prospect of a Trump presidency mounted in September 2016 when he sat down for an interview.

> I'm coming from a country where you don't have any political rights, except to elect the same party all the time. You're allowed to vote but only for one candidate. There's no choice. But here in America, I've seen a lot of people aren't supporting the democracy the way it should be. They are

just so hyper-critical with the government, about the political system. I will take them to Cuba and let them be Cuban citizens for just six months and I'm pretty sure when they come back they would see things very differently. Democracy, I acknowledge, is not the best way of governing. But I would say the good things outweigh the bad things: the freedom to be able to speak about whatever you want; the opportunity to choose from at least two candidates; to be free to be affiliated with a political party; to share your political feelings without fear of being overlooked or checked or chased. That's amazing. This is what I was expecting from America. That's why I came here. Freedom.

But democracy only works with culture. If you don't have culture, democracy won't work. There's no way. There's a saying from José Martí, "You must be cultured in order to be free." If you don't have an education you can be manipulated.

Many people aren't getting an education in Syracuse, which is really a systemic problem because sometimes it is a vicious circle. You've grown up like your family or your neighbors or your friends and you just can't come out of that. Sometimes you realize that when you're in big trouble. Then it's too late. So you have to go back and keep doing bad things. It's basically that.

It's very sad, especially in the high schools. The students feel like they're men and sometimes they're completely wrong. They don't know anything. They are out of touch with every sensible decision. That's sad. It's always easier to blame the government, to blame others. You have to be bold enough to recognize your own faults. That's my opinion. For example, I had an alcoholic father. It traumatized my childhood. But once I gained consciousness about myself, do you think I could blame my father for what he did or what he didn't do to me? No. It's my responsibility. That's all.

Sometimes you'll hear in Syracuse, "Those white people, they did this to us. They have us segregated, marginalized, we don't have good jobs." But that's not the point. The point is you're responsible. Once you reach thirteen years old, you have your self-awareness, your self-consciousness. It's your decision. It's not your father's decision. It's not your grandfather's decision.

One thing I really have to acknowledge: in Cuba we don't blame each other. Every racial group, we don't blame each other for the problems. In Cuba, you're measured by what you are. That's wonderful stuff. That's something very valuable. There is always some bias against black people, but that's happening at a very low percentage. Mostly, we go to the same schools. There are no private schools. All are public schools. Really you don't see the difference between a black boy and white boy. That's something good. It's fair. It's the

same to get your engineering, medical degrees:
you have to be smart. You have to have the abilities to get that. The only skin color that can pre-
vent you from going to the university is not to be
in accord with the government. That's the only
skin color problem.

Being from outside, you can see both sides of
the coin. My philosophy is take the best of both
worlds. I will embrace the American values that
really are the best without giving up on my Cuban
values that I consider good ones. I wouldn't give
up that, never. I have a certain advantage over
you because I have that second point of view. But
I really love the American values.

Though Justo worked hard to understand and adopt
the American ways, no assimilation could be complete without his family members. Their passage
from Cuba was caught up in the slow churn of immigration bureaucracy. He yearned to see them
much sooner than the process would allow, so, surprisingly, he plotted to return to Cuba for a visit.

The very idea of a refugee returning to his or
her native country seemed to be sheer lunacy.
Why go back to the nation you've fled? Won't you
be detained indefinitely by the regime that once
repressed you? Many newly-minted Syracusans
who were delivered to the city after enduring war,
torture, and crowded refugee camps would never

dream of tempting fate in that way. Only prison could wait.

Yet Justo wanted to see his family. And he knew the risks of slipping back into Cuba were few. You see, as perverse as it may sound, Cuba welcomed refugees for brief visits home. Or better put, welcomed the American dollars that refugees brought home.

The Raúl Castro government had modified travel laws to allow Cubans who have left to return home as many times as they like within two years after their initial departure. Expatriates could spend Cuban pesos on their first visit home but thereafter had to show their greenbacks. For Justo, it was like a gold-embossed invitation.

"It's hard to describe," he said in English that is only rarely halting.

> Outside you're happy because you're seeing your family—your wife, your children, your mother—and your land, your friends, your people, the place where you were born. That's very important. On the other hand, you know you are helping the regime by bringing money back in. That's the truth.
>
> Also, I feel very sad because I've seen more poverty, and values are deteriorating very fast. I'd say since 2014 until today, what's going on is a stampede, a lot of people trying to get out of the country by whatever means. That's sad because

usually the smartest people go first and then after that all that remains is the crap. You can see it on the streets. When you walk through the streets you see the buildings fall apart. The way the people speak, the way they treat each other. The values are going down very, very fast—the respect, the good manners, the politeness, the courtesy. All of that is going down. When I was a boy it was different. Right now, I don't see that. I don't know what's going on, really. I don't want to imagine what will happen once the regime goes down.

So if the regime goes down, there won't be a capable leadership class to take its place. The "crap" he refers to may be the only recourse. And, ironically, he and other educated Cubans here in Syracuse and the rest of the United States who are enriching this nation and working jobs that some Americans won't take will watch from afar, torn, perhaps, but reluctant to go back.

Over on the southwest side of Syracuse, the day retreated toward dinnertime when a late-model sedan slipped onto a narrow service road running behind a row of the neatly painted Dutch colonial homes so common in the neighborhood. Stopping behind a house whose tall backyard fence was perfect cover for late afternoon delight, the driver lit up two joints, and he and his girlfriend eased their seats back and shimmied out of their clothing. Outside the car, the aroma of grilled chicken and roasted vegetables drifted from a nearby home. The competing smell of burning marijuana rousted Trevor Russell, a divorced carpenter who lives in his sister's house.[1] He peeked from his attic window, spied the unfamiliar Honda, and dashed downstairs and into the alley.

Trevor counts himself among the protectors of the neighborhood, like the retired cops and frequent dog walkers who have 911 on speed dial. However, Trevor rarely calls the police. He's an Army vet who dreams of living off the grid, happy to settle matters for himself rather than rely on society's institutions. The late urbanist Jane Jacobs might have called him a "public character," as much for his unconventional outlook as the protection he provides.

Trevor tapped on the car window just as the occupants were settling in, signaling that they better move on. The driver yanked his pants to his waist and burst from the car, firing off a fierce round of expletives and accusations that Trevor returned in full measure. Neighbors clambered away from their kitchen tables and kids abandoned their ball games just in time to see the stranger land a punch across their defender's chin.

1. The name "Trevor Russell" is a pseudonym.

The driver dashed back to his car and was grop-
ing for his keys when Trevor, stumbling to regain
his footing, reached for a large rock on the side of
the road and heaved it toward the car.

Time stood still on that humid afternoon. Like a
large black bird riding a friendly updraft, the rock
sailed through the air and then dove toward the
ground, glancing off the front door. The driver looked
through his window in astonishment. Warned by a
neighbor that the police were on their way, he sped
off, his last audible words concerning the rental
agency that owned the car.

Trevor's sister led him toward home.

The neighborhood defender grew up about 15 miles
outside Syracuse in the 1960s and '70s, speeding
into the city when he got his driver's license to buy
Doors and Stevie Wonder records at a store somewhere between the old 15th Ward and Syracuse
University. In 1976, he graduated high school and
joined the army. By the 1980s, he was married and
living in New England, learning the construction
trade and volunteering as an EMT where, presumably, he could burn off his drive to step up for his
fellow man, like in the alley.

After his marriage broke up, Trevor chose to return
to Syracuse, where a series of property managers

engaged him to repair and keep up houses, many of them forever on the edge of being condemned. His work plopped him down right in the middle of the city's pathetic housing market in which some buyers, many of them from faraway places like California, England, and Japan, scoop up inexpensive houses, pay for minimal updates, and rent them to poor city dwellers, including newly arrived immigrants.

Trevor's employers take care of the properties for the absentee landowners for 10 percent of the cost of rent. In addition, they oversee their own rental properties, hoping that their client business pays the upkeep on those investments. His bosses also find themselves using their collections from clients to pay for urgent repairs to other clients' homes, setting up a hopeless cycle that often leaves them the victim of deadbeat landlords who refuse to part with 10 percent of the rent. Many of the absentee landlords, said Trevor, have been snookered themselves.

You had this program for years whereby people were advertising in Europe and Asia, "Buy properties in America for pennies on the dollar and rent them out for $600 a month. There's two apartments in this house. You get $1,200 a month . . . Your mortgage is $600 a month. You clear $600 a month, free and clear." And that's all they tell them, so they buy the house. Well, the house needs $60,000 worth of work to pass code. They don't tell them that. They don't tell them that the taxes are in arrears for "x" number of dollars. So these people end up with these houses. One guy finally came into town, and I thought he was going to cry. I showed him all the work I had done just to fix the structure and the place was still a shithole. And all I had done was replace all of the substructure framing that had been put in. We weren't even to the Sheetrock stage yet. They were scammed. These people were buying these properties, thinking they're going to make a million dollars in the real estate market and they're buying inner city properties that have huge problems. And they don't know it. The photographs look great. They don't know that the place hasn't been rented in five years . . . or just one apartment's been rented in five years and the roof leaks and this and that. It's preying on people's greed.

But that's the landlord's problem, and Trevor's. Sitting in his garage, next to a glistening Harley-Davidson roadster, the Brickyard 400 droning on a nearby television, he recounted that his problems are on the frontlines of the housing economy, in the hallways, bathrooms, and neighborhoods where he makes repairs.

I've seen apartments that dogs have completely destroyed. They didn't just chew on the woodwork;

the pitbulls have ripped the woodwork off of the door casings, ripped the doors off the kitchen cabinets, ripped the stiles out of the cabinets, destroyed the doors. These are dogs that have been trained to fight.

One day, I'm out in front of a place that I'm working on. I was waiting for the water department to come by and put the meter in. People steal the meters on the buildings. They ripped all the copper out, so I had to go in and do all new PEX throughout the building. And they'd stolen the meter. I was waiting for the water department and one of the guys from across the street comes running from behind his house and there's two dogs chasing him, so I jump up in the back of my pickup truck. He's trying to get into the back of the truck, and I'm smacking the dogs and smacking the dogs and finally the dogs take off. And the dog officers come and take the dogs and two weeks later they give the dogs back. The dogs lived on the street—they were a nuisance to everybody, everybody came out and told the dog officer when he took them that they were a nuisance. I just don't get it.

I went into one refugee apartment one day and somebody had spray-painted on the door, "Get the fuck out. You don't belong here." Welcome to America. You go upstairs and there's a sofa and you start counting the adults. There's the middle-aged couple with the kids and there's two sets of elderly people . . . his parents and her parents. And then there's an aunt or an uncle who comes by from time to time and actually speaks English and tells you what needs to be done, interprets for you. Or you got to wait for the kids to get out of school. It got to the point where I would get a work order and I'd say, "I'm going to this one at 3:00. You got it down at 11:00, but I'm going later because the kids will be home from school. They speak English. They can interpret for me."

On the North Side, when you work on an apartment rented by immigrants, you don't go hungry because you start working and they fire up the stove. And the next thing you know you got a plate of rice in front of you. When I did a Korean's place, I'm upstairs putting the last window in and I turn around and she's got a tray with enough food for ten people! You go to the South Side and they say, "When are you going to be done . . . hurry up and fix that . . . how come that's broken."

You got immigrants who play the same thing as the people who think they're entitled. They learn the system right away, a lot of them. Most of those people are educated; they're from India, Pakistan, Iran. If they were born any place in world, they'd still be that way. They'd stop paying the rent and they'd know exactly when the marshal would come. We'd say, "We sent you a notice of eviction. You're supposed to be out." They'd say, "You've got to get the marshal to come take me out, and it takes 45 days from the eviction notice to the marshal coming." Of course, they're not going to pay rent for those 45 days. Sometimes the marshal comes and they're gone. Sometimes the marshal comes and they're still living there and they get pissed and they destroy the inside of the place. They super glue the locks on the meter, so the guy from the utility company couldn't turn off the electricity. They would disconnect the water meter from the pipe and let the water run into the cellar.

But there are even more pathetic things. Unattended babies walking down the sidewalk with a loaded diaper. Seven in the morning, you're on the way to work, fortunately your sister works at social services so you pull up on the curb next to the kid and you call her and say, "I got a two-year-old walking down the sidewalk with a diaper full of poop." She says, "Drive away." You say, "What?" She says, "Drive away. Go down the block and stop where you can see the kid in your mirror." So I go down the block and stop. She says, "I've already called the police." Somebody might come out of the house and shoot you, if you start talking to that kid . . . or might come out and beat you up because the mother's now going to be charged with negligence that the kid's out alone and she's going to try to blame you, that you tried to grab up her kid. In a minute, the cop came flipping around the corner and I waved at him and he waved at me as he went by. I could see the mother outside of the house screaming when the cop came around the corner.

8

✧ ✧ ✧

PROCEED
TO GO

The neglected child Trevor Russell witnessed on the street is the kind of tragedy that enrages Elise Baker and haunts her dreams. Last night, she twitched and rolled under the covers of her bed as scenes from her neighborhood flashed and then faded: cracked sidewalks, desolate streets, sad corner stores, idle men on sagging front porches, and houses devoid of life. But then the ethereal picture segued to paved roads, planters on corners brimming with flowers, men walking with purpose to jobs, houses freshly painted and alive with mothers and fathers and children.

A few weeks ago, after another night of restlessness, she had risen and gathered a few friends for a prayerful pincer movement against the blight and dissipation of her city. It was spiritual warfare, Elise Baker style. "I said to them, 'Come downtown and meet me because we have to put a covenant over these young people down here and we need to pray around.' We went around by where all the young people are and over by the Rescue Mission and I'm praying in the name of Jesus, 'God bless them, take away their desire for drugs.' By the time I was so filled with it, I left all of my friends. I was on a mission. I want to make change. But that change inside of me is such a thing that it sometimes promotes wrong."

Sitting in the downtown public library where security guards were waking up vagrant people who had fallen asleep, Elise dabbed her tears. She confessed to playing numbers to raise money for her dreams of community renewal. Harmless in the eyes of the tens of thousands of her fellow New Yorkers who daily buy lottery tickets, it is a failure of faith in her mind, a pitfall of the very streets she seeks to renew and an endorsement of the corner stores in her neighborhood that also sell malt liquor and sugar-soaked foods. Her noble intent makes no difference.

But it's not just the numbers that pained her. On other nights, she imagined the faces of young nephews, cousins, and foster children whom she had counseled in the name of the golden rule who had fallen into drug dealing. "These young people are people I have raised in the first three years of their life. Their parents were not doing the right things. I remember one of my foster children said to me, 'Mom, you made us want to help people. It's inside of me so bad that I'm just trying to deal dope to get money to help other people.' Did I push helping too much to where it promoted wrongfulness? They want to always help people, which they got from me. So I blame myself, and I don't like the fact that they don't see no way out other than to sell drugs. I was trying to teach them to community build, not destroy the community."

In the library, an unsteady man with rheumy eyes interrupted Elise. They know each other from the in-school suspension halls she supervised. "I'm gettin' it together. I'm gettin' it together," he repeated. The young man darted away while Elise shook her head. "He's got to get off drugs," she whispered.

As misplaced as Elise's guilt seems, her thoughts about young men on drugs point out one significant reality in the city of Syracuse. The pull among young black males to sell drugs is undeniable. Virtually every person in that demographic must make the decision, at one time or another, whether or not to deal. It's an acceptable way to make a living in wide swaths of the Syracuse street culture, and thrives in the absence of jobs and family pressures that might otherwise deter.

Like many of those for whom Elise prays, Stefon
Greene flirted with street-corner life. In middle
school, after years of living with his grandmother
Willa, he had moved back with his mother, Debra,
who was living in a small house on the South Side.
In the years since the separation from her son,
she had married and gone through numerous re-
habs, but young Stefon soon discovered she was
far from clean. "It was tough," he said. "I was dealing with things that I'd never seen before. I was
having experiences and meeting people that I had
never come in contact with, people who my mom
knew and her friends." He took advantage of her
addiction, knowing that it was always easier to get
a "yes" when she was high or feeling guilty about
getting high. He began staying out all night and
running around with kids who lived on the edge
of gang life.

Many mornings, he slipped past the living room
couch where Debra had collapsed and walked in
the opposite direction of his middle school. By high
school, he played hooky two of every three days.
Letters home from the school district were barely
comprehensible to his mother, who now—because
her second husband, Stefon's stepfather, was frequently out of work—had been forced to relocate
to the Pioneer Homes public housing community

just down the hill from Syracuse University and near Interstate 81.[1]

While Stefon sampled street life around the Pioneer Homes, his mother floundered. She had begun snorting cocaine in the 1970s when she met Stefon's father, who was a dealer. She'd steal a few hits from his retail supply, but she brushed away the powder when she encountered crack, which decimated the using community in the 1980s, claiming lives and sending dealers to prison for long stretches. The hard-hitting drug made national headlines in 1986 when University of Maryland basketball player Len Bias, on the eve of a promising career with the Boston Celtics, died after smoking it.

Recently, Debra sipped a bottle of water in a downtown coffee shop and recalled her first taste. "This girl I knew from a long time ago, she was telling me something about cooking drugs. Her and her husband invited me over and we sitting there having drinks and he has this glass rocker and he was putting stuff in there and I was sipping on my gin—I was drinking gin back then. I said, 'What's that?' She said, 'This is a crack pipe.' He had this funny-shaped glass thing and he put the crack rock in there and told me to pull. The smoke was going all around in it . . . and that was it. I was always trying to chase that first feeling after that, and I never

1. Many Syracusans refer to Pioneer Homes as the "P-H."

found it. I never felt it again. Everybody that's gotten high off crack will tell you the same thing.

"It became a job," she said. "I knew things was out of hand because I would get up in the morning and get cleaned up and do everything I was supposed to do and then I would start thinking about how am I going to get some money to get high. And that might start at three or four in the afternoon. And then we was on a roll all night until the next morning until I finally got tired and laid down to go to sleep."

Meanwhile, against a wicked cacophony of gunfire and roaring traffic from the nearby I-81 highway, Stefon continued to explore the Pioneer Homes freedom that his mother's addiction afforded him. "It's gang territory," he said. "There are kids who grew up with a ton of guys who are in gangs and live their whole life in the Pioneer Homes and now are either in gangs or in jail. I started hanging with them. We did some things that almost got me arrested." Like the night they crept up to Marshall Street, the small commercial district that serves the university community, with an eye on stealing sneakers. There were too many people hanging around the store to pull off their caper, so they got the idea to mug somebody with a BB gun. "One of the kids does it, and we all run down to the P-H, and I go home like normal and I remember changing my clothes and going to sit on the porch and that's when all of the police came in front of the house, a lot of police cars. They pulled us all off the porch and they stood us up and they had the guy in the back of the car and luckily he couldn't identify us."

If not robbery, then drug dealing promised the key to new sneakers. He began selling marijuana. "We were young, thirteen or fourteen years old, and at that age you have to be on the streets. You don't have a car. You're standing out on a corner some-where waiting for a five-dollar or ten-dollar sale. I was nowhere in a place that you see in the movies. If I had to classify it as a novice or an expert, I was way below novice. We were just knuckleheads try-ing to be in a lifestyle that could take us somewhere very bad. Personally for me it was hard to live that life. I was also trying to do it at a time when my mom was still using."

Stefon resented the dealers who fed his mother's habit, so his own attempts to sell plagued him. But not enough to stop him. "Maybe when I was fourteen or fifteen, I started trying to sell cocaine and stuff. It was up until that point that I wouldn't do it because I thought about my mother. But you have all those peers around you and all those peo-ple who point you in one direction, so you think this is the best way to make money. Until you re-alize that you're not making money. You have the same amount of money. You're spending the same sixty or a hundred dollars over and over again and you haven't gotten anywhere. And I wasn't getting anywhere."

Over the years, Stefon's father often whisked him away as he went on his rounds to visit bars and girl-friends. Stefon has no memory of his parents ever living together, but his father never disappeared from his life, although recollections of his appear-ances often stir mixed emotions.

Their travels throughout the side streets and bou-levards of the South Side often wound up at gambling houses, which have dotted black neighborhoods in Syracuse ever since there were black neighbor-hoods in Syracuse. Set up in the front parlors of nondescript homes or the back rooms of quiet bars, they have been the scenes of small fortunes won and lost, knife attacks, and marathon poker games that tested the manhood, if not the endurance, of their players. Naturally, they spawned an Old West mythology in the neighborhoods of Syracuse as well as in the precinct houses of police who either busted them or looked the other way, according to how busy their shifts were or how handsome the payoffs.

Stefon never witnessed any showdowns, but he spent his share of afternoons and evenings hanging around card games whenever his father—whose own mother ran a gambling house—took a notion to try his luck. He thinks he tagged along for the first time at the age of ten. "If he sits at the table, we could be there for three hours," explained Stefon. "If it was a Saturday in the summertime I was fine, I could go outside, there was kids around. This would be in a neighborhood that I wasn't used to, so I was playing with kids I didn't know. That would be fun. But other times it would be in the evening and there'd be nothing to do. Now that I think about it, I was just there. There was just a table and couch in there and all those old people playing cards. That was interesting. I always remember my father saying, 'All right, I got to drop you off now. It's grown folks' time.' That meant he was going off to a bar or to a girlfriend."

Stefon's older brother, Glen, had little patience for his father's raffish ways. The old man attempted to sell him lemon cars and had given him little attention. But Stefon clung to his father's redeeming qualities. "There was one summer I lived with my mother when she lived on the South Side and this was when my mother was really drinking a lot, and she was still on drugs. I noticed him come around more compared to when I lived with my grandmother, where I had everything I needed. But when I stayed with my mom, he knew the lifestyle there, so he realized that he had to check on me more."

Even in the wake of a brutal fight between his father and his stepfather, he chose to see his father's charm. "My stepfather and my mom had a long weekend of drinking," he recalled.

At this point I was just trying to push myself away from that. Be gone more, be with my friends more, spend my nights at as many friends as I could to get out of that situation. But I got a call in the early morning. My mom and my stepdad were having an argument that turned into a fight. When they would get in an argument, me and two of my best friends would always go to my stepdad threatening to beat him up. So I guess at this point my stepdad attempted to defend himself against me. I called my dad. There have been times when I've called him and he said he was coming to pick me up and never came. But this was the fastest he's ever responded to any of my calls. He came there, and he wanted to know what's going on and they got in this big argument. He punched my stepdad a few times. It was this big thing. The police were called, and my stepdad said, "The police are here now but we'll remember this." I remember my dad saying to him, "Okay, Travis. We'll see when the police are gone." Then, maybe seven months later, my dad's at our house and they're drinking and stuff and partying. I'm young. But my dad looks at my stepdad very cordially and says with a smile as he laughs, "You know, I remember what you said to me that day with the police, and you said you wouldn't forget. I didn't forget either, but we'll let it go now."

If Stefon witnessed street life from the point of view of the street, Jessi Lyons saw it through her Portland vision as she set up urban living in service of an urban dream of coexistence and sustainability. If it could happen in the Northwest then why not in Syracuse? Her husband wasn't so sure, particularly after finally learning of the threats and thefts near the okra and sunflowers. But he had agreed with Jessi that sending their twins to public school was the community-friendly thing to do. That was in September of 2016.

By November, Trump was the president-elect and Jessi's husband was beginning to see city life as a form of resistance to the reactionary new leader. Said Jessi, "He's a lot more comfortable here than he is with our other options. For us it's not an option of stay in Syracuse or go to a suburb. It's stay in Syracuse or go.

"He's a scientist. People are saying climate change isn't real and science shouldn't be supported so his livelihood as a scientist is threatened. He's studying biofuels! All funding is going to be cut functionally for research that he does now. He just got a PhD in something that's going to be pretty much absent unless we have a major political shift soon. His best chances of employment right now are in Germany."

Whether or not a choice between Syracuse or Germany loomed in the future, Jessi and her husband walked their children to the nearby school, where they saw poor children arriving late and missing the free breakfast that they probably needed. On the way back home, after dropping off their kids, they saw other children even further behind the clock, staring at the ground, refusing to acknowledge hellos, hardened at their tender age. "My husband has talked about understanding the neighborhood dynamic more and the value of it," continued Jessi. "While our kids sometimes hate having to walk to and from school, it's a chance to monitor other kids and be with them. He gets that and it helps to balance that fear and being demoralized by crime in the city."

About the time their children started the school year, it was pretty easy to be "demoralized by crime in the city." In late August, somebody heaved a chunk of asphalt through the front window of Jessi's home. Then a gang of young teens terrorized her block.

This group of middle schoolers was walking up Midland and Salina, and they were chucking rocks on a daily basis at cars that were driving by, and one woman actually got in a severe accident from it because it broke her windshield while she was driving and she went into a telephone pole. This is 3:00 p.m. traffic on Salina and then our other neighbor a few houses down . . . the group chased her husband in her own yard and were hurling large rocks at him and the next time they chased their eight-year-old daughter with rocks. This had been allowed to continue by the police because these things were happening during a shift change and they weren't telling each other about it. So I went to a neighborhood meeting and talked to somebody at the police department and finally got our neighborhood police to address it. It was four months into this issue when the police finally show up at our door, wanting more information, saying "This is the first we've heard of it." This is our neighborhood police! We had made a report and sent video made by our neighbors, who actually got the kids on video, at least a dozen reports. They would stand at our driveway, and we would be there unable to do anything and they did not care.

It finally resolved right before winter came because one of the kids was caught on a much worse crime. He had stolen a car, crashed it and had a gun and so he was kind of the ringleader. That was a big deal for us but also got more neighbors involved. We're talking about creating a neighborhood watch for our block. In some ways it's good because it brought more interests together and got more neighbors talking.

More danger also spilled into the farm. A young employee named Terrence Newley had lost his motorbike to thieves and tracked it down a few days later, but the group who had stolen it came looking for him, lurking in the woods across from the farm until Jessi and a volunteer left to go to a meeting.[2] Immediately, they sprang on him, slashing him with knives and wresting his keys from him. Jessi said that Terrence identified the teens on social media, but the police failed to follow up when he contacted them.

Terrence had come into Jessi's world some five years earlier when both were helping out with other fledgling urban farms around the South Side. "I remember him because I was pregnant with my twins and he was seventeen and had year-old twins and a three-year-old. I was very fond of him. He had this great personality and was driven. Then . . . I was given the assignment of taking a family to a community breakfast and it was Terrence's family. So we chatted, and he said he'd love to get back to urban farming." As the Brady Farm took root in the spring of 2016, they met again while Jessi was planning the farm with Brady staff. Terrence, a regular

2. The name "Terrence Newley" is a pseudonym.

around the Brady Faith Center, stumbled into the building after being held by police for a week as a witness to his own shooting. He had been clipped while leaving a party and when a suspect had been arrested, police picked him up while on his way to collect his kids from the bus stop and held him until he could testify against the assailant. Explained Jessi, "His own father said, 'How dare you go to the police with this? How dare you snitch?' There was a community repercussion for him, that he was a snitch, because he participated in justice for himself, by his own family. He is so driven to contribute. He's really creative. He's very bright, but he dropped out of school."

Still, Jessi was hooked. She asked him to join the farm's full-time staff in the spring of 2016, funding half of his position through a subsidy from an employment services agency for county residents on welfare, this despite his deep lack of skills. "I didn't realize how little education he accomplished until a recent community gathering when I gave him three sentences to read in front of people and he couldn't read the word 'eight.' And many of the words that were pretty basic he couldn't do. Just this week I asked him to send out an email and it was clear that he couldn't do basic word processing."

But that was the point. The farm's mission includes workforce development and mentoring, so despite his deficits, Terrence made for an ideal candidate, particularly when Jessi factored in his drive to succeed. "He's my partner in crime, partner in justice," said Jessi.

> He's great. We're kind of going through a lot together and it's been good for me as somebody who has to employ people. I'm so glad I'm working for Brady because I'm in a position to do this. Any other position I had, I would have fired Terrence ages ago. I never would have hired him to begin with. His drastic lack of skills and experience and exposure to any level of professional experience outside of flipping burgers is so lacking that somebody has to help him because he has so much to offer. He's really frustrated because he knows he's being held back. He doesn't know he should have been using spell-check, easy things. So he's really been struggling. Anyway, my relationship with him as a mentor is trying to get him in touch with these things. His first job is to get his driver's license by April 1. He's still trying to take some tests and get his GED, and, by the end of this growing season, he needs to be functional in Excel and Word. He needs to be able to update the website. Part of structuring our employment, I had to sacrifice hiring people from the community, so I could have skilled people that are trainable. I'm not able to train everybody at everything and make the farm function. Instead I need

people who have skills who can help me mentor everybody else that we're hiring, so I can spend the time really helping Terrence to get where he needs to be in a meaningful way. So that I can continue employing him.

9

✧ ✧ ✧

TEMPTATION

Back in high school, Stefon Greene needed the same kind of attention Terrence Newley would receive at the Brady Farm in 2016: Stefon was chronically absent from classes and on the verge of banishment from the city schools, which could only lead to a lifetime in and out of the criminal justice system. When he did go to school, he showed up for second period but slept through it and then attended all three lunch sittings before skipping the rest of the day. A friend who had received an $80,000 settlement after being hit by a car had bought his own car, so Stefon cruised with him and spent most nights at his friend's house to avoid the bedlam in his mother's home.

"I always point back to that and realize I could have been a totally different person. I could be in

jail right now," he said. At the time, he was disappointing the vision of his grandparents, failing to
take advantage of the possibilities they had created
by coming to Syracuse in the first place.

Grandfather Ted's death in 1992 had left his
wife, Willa, in confusion. Stefon had moved in with
her when his mother could no longer function as a
parent, but she began to show early signs of Alz-
heimer's disease and, as her health declined, she
had no choice but to let him go back to his mother,
Debra. Fortunately, Debra's brother Rob stepped
in to provide stability where Debra and now Willa
could not. "My wife and I don't have any kids," recalled Rob.

We just took to Stefon. We wanted to show him
that you have a choice: go this way and this is
what's going to happen. He's definitely seen the
bad but we made sure he saw some good in the
world, that there's good people out there.

He's a smart kid. We saw that early on. Everybody saw that. It was like, "Ok. He's going to get
it." And he did. From the bad things he saw, he
saw how bad they were and he didn't want to go
that way. The good things he saw made him feel
good, made him realize, "Hey, I don't have to be
in so much pain on this side of it all the time. I can
make good in the world." If I had an influence, I'm
glad. That makes me more than happy.

At the time, Stefon was a growing boy. He was confused about his mother, but not wanting to be with his mother. I remember there was one time that he was staying with her that the police came and tore the house apart. He was a kid and he was seeing all this stuff. So he went back with my mom, back to the house, and he would just act out. It was hard for my mother to deal with that, after a while. So we were really struggling through that time. My sister was in and out of everything. We tried to keep Stefon in school, which we did. My mother was very instrumental in that. When he said he didn't feel like going to school, she'd say, "You're getting up and you're going somewhere." She did the same thing to us.

As my mom got worse, he made the jump to go with his mother; it was very, very different. With his grandmother, the house was a safe haven. When he got with his mom, things were happening, and we'd take him for the weekend. My wife would make sure that she'd have something planned. He had a friend who lived where we lived and they were both the same age, so we'd have them both over and they could stay at the house. We could take him places, camping, to get him a little bit away from his mom's world. That was a very hard and confusing time. His dad was in and out of his life. It just wasn't good. That was the time that we were most worried about which

way he would go. What he was seeing, where he
was going. But he stayed in school. When he had
a math problem, he'd call me up or ask my wife.

"Uncle Rob's got to be the biggest male figure in my
life," said Stefon.

Everything I am now is probably because of his
example, seeing him with his wife, seeing how
he treated my grandmother, seeing how he does
those things and lives a regular life outside of the
struggles that people have on the South Side or
outside the regular black struggles. He was the
first black man I seen that lived outside all that
stuff and he was the first black man I've ever met
to accept being different: he played rock music
and had rock bands and had a white wife.

They showed me all these other things about
the world that I would have never ever seen and
it was awesome. My aunt Ann [Rob's wife] taught
me the simple things that are so important to life
as an adult. We would go into restaurants and
she'd say, "Say thank you to the waitress." Or,
"Say please when you ask for something." There's
one time when we were in a store when I was
very little and I took a piece of gum out of the
store. And she caught me chewing it in the car
and she asked me where I got the gum from and
then she gave me this whole thing about stealing

and not stealing and she would give me anything I wanted. And I still remember it because as simple as it is I know I can't go into a place and take whatever I want. Sad to say some young kids today at 16 and 17 years old don't think like that. They feel like it's okay to have a gun and shoot people on the street and not take life into consideration.

Stefon's older brother, Glen, also took an interest. No angel, the brother knew his share of street life as a teenager, but he walked away from trouble in manhood. He never let Stefon forget about his innate intelligence, pointing him always to better horizons. "He was good about standing up to my mom and my stepdad about the wrong they were doing and not trying to project that stuff on me. All he wanted me to do was be in school. I dropped out of Corcoran High School twice, and he took me back there both times and said, 'You're not dropping out of school. There's no point.' He got in a huge argument with the principal about getting me back in school. Nobody wanted to let me back in school."

During the turbulence of Stefon's middle- and high-school years, he met Elise Baker, who at the time worked in various enrichment and remediation programs in the Syracuse City School District. Like Glen and Uncle Rob, she kept an eye on him. In eighth grade, he found himself in an intervention program for youths heading toward a life of crime. "But he didn't belong there only because he was such a jovial person," said Elise. "It seems like he didn't fit the qualifications of the at-risk programs because he was a happy-go-lucky person. He was silly. But he was trying to fit in with other people, that gang-banger type."

"My transition from elementary to middle school was tough," said Stefon. "It was a whole transitioning in my life that was happening. That same year I had gone from living with my grandmother for seven years to living with my mom full time. I moved to the South Side from the East Side. Life at my grandma's house was totally different from life with my mom. I had a lot of privileges with my mother. She would let a lot of things go. Now I realize it was the first time me and her had lived together since I was five years old. A lot of it was her making sure that I was going to be OK. But then it turned into me not doing what I was supposed to do. She would let a lot of it go."

In the after-school program that Elise helped run, the students studied African dance, poetry, printing, and leather-working. "We went into their mindset to try to pull out the gifts and the talents that were in them," she said. "We took them to places that they never would have had the chance to go to."

When high school started, Stefon landed in another evening program that was little different from the other, only that, there, Elise was in charge. "As long as he was with me there were certain things that I would stay on him about," she said. "His problem was with his associations. He got entangled in the streets for a while. And it probably has to do with puberty and boys trying to be men and all the other stuff that goes with it."

Only he was developing a late-teen edge, landing in Corcoran High School's in-school suspension (ISS) again and again, where Elise was also working. But when Stefon showed up at school one morning with a box cutter like many of his friends carried around, he was assigned to a homebound program, which would finally shepherd him to graduation.

Elise's relationship with ISS would prove more complicated, not surprisingly. "ISS wasn't developed properly to me, so what I did was change it," she said. "The students would normally go in there and sit, laugh, comb their hair, and do nothing. I didn't understand this. These kids come in here and it's like a rest stop for them. I tried to change it, so every time they came in there they had to write fifty sentences: 'My education is important. I will not return to ISS.' I raised the number each time so it would be tormenting to them, so they wouldn't want to come back there. I had them write essays and then correct them and had them write it over again." If the kids goofed off, she'd collar them, jack them up. To which Stefon can attest. "She used to pop us in the back of the head," he recalled.

She'd quiz them about their behavior, and call home when they were thrown into her classroom. But the administration tolerated none of it, she said, demanding that she merely babysit the students when they came her way.

The job ended when she confronted a few white students who lived in the neighborhood around the high school. Their trip into the nearby woods to smoke pot ended in a visit to ISS, where they hoped to sleep it off. "I wouldn't let them, I don't care how high you are. You're going to stay up. Sometimes I would squirt them with a water bottle and get them up, but it was out of love. I wasn't trying to hurt anybody. They were Caucasians compared to the 80 percent black in ISS, but each white child I scorned the same way I would have done any black child. In this case, I called the parents and I told them that the students were in there and they were high. One of those parents was related to the principal, so when I called them they called him. They took my phones out of the room after that. They said, 'You don't do this!' I still made the calls, at home."

Elise quietly moved on to another school. But not before leaving her mark on Stefon Greene. "Miss Baker is somebody who is really pro-religion and pro-black all at the same time. When she called me a couple of weeks ago, I was telling her that I have a

new boss, and she's like, 'Don't ever say "boss," because "boss" goes back to slavery.' She still thinks
so critically about those things and that's why I ap-
preciate her. I'll keep saying it, but now when I say
it I'll think about that. I was lucky to start those
programs with Miss Baker and have something to
do after school. If I could say there's any solution
to inner city violence, especially with young people
involved in crime, it is that they need something to
do with their idle time."

As much as Stefon counts Elise and Uncle Rob
as saviors, he created his own turning point in high
school and then college. Wary of the pull of drugs,
he set out one Saturday for the bleak commercial
drag on the rim of town called Erie Boulevard, determined to keep walking along the road until he
found a job. He stepped into the Krispy Kreme
donut shop and left as a baker, replacing a man
who'd lost his finger on the job. But Stefon held on
to his digits and over the next few years worked in
a grocery store and restaurants that kept him away
from the still-alluring drug sales.

In 2007, Stefon graduated from high school and
entered Onondaga Community College, where he
showed his academic potential but struggled to
shake the urge to sell drugs. His friends on campus

talked about the good cash they made peddling marijuana and coke, and back at Pioneer Homes, where he lived with his mother, he noted the dealers' sneakers and brand new sedans. "If you're selling a big drug like heroin or crack cocaine," he said, "you're spending most of your nights partying with people and you're making a ton of money and you have all these things that you need, and you have all the independence. You don't have to be anywhere. You don't have to be at work in the morning. You don't have to do this and don't have to do that."

Even after he moved on to a four-year school, the nearby Le Moyne College, where his grandparents had cleaned floors and bathrooms, drugs still pulled hard, like when dealer friends bragged about their fat billfolds. "I remember reading in philosophy class about how doing the right thing is always harder. It makes a lot of sense because doing the right thing *is* always harder, but it was hard for me to step out of that mindset. It was hard for me to realize that I'm around my friends and people that they know and they're like, 'I got this money and then I'll buy an ounce and then I'll flip it and then I'll be straight.' I understand the attraction fully. It's not as illogical as people think."

It was romance of a different kind that finally stanched the temptation: his girlfriend Naureen. When he met her in high school, he was still selling weed but she didn't like the girls who bought from him, so he quit.

I was lucky enough to meet a girl who didn't want her boyfriend to be a part of that stuff. A lot of me stopping being in the streets was also because of her. My mother let her stay with us anytime she wanted to, so why be in the streets? I didn't need to. I had a girlfriend at home. It was Memorial Day of 2007 when she got hit by a car. She broke her leg. We were at a family barbecue. It was the first time she had met my father's side of the family. Her mother and my mother agreed that it would be OK for her to stay with us. My mother had always had my brothers at home and they always had their girlfriends living with them. But they were living that same type of lifestyle that my mom was living. But we weren't. I told Naureen the other day, because of her she changed the whole dynamic of my family.

It just happened to be around the same time that my mom had this revelation in herself and said, "I can't keeping doing this." This was after a few times she had relapsed. My mom had always tried to stop doing drugs and stop drinking alcohol, but never wanted to go to any inpatient rehab. The last time she finally did an outpatient where she would go to the program every day, it wasn't mandated by any court. She had decided to do it. Then it all went uphill. She decided to go back to school and get her GED.

Then Debra earned a college degree, satisfied that she had left behind that other life. "Drugs just take everything from a family," she said. "They take your soul. Me and Stefon were so far apart, I didn't give it much thought because all I was thinking about was drinking and getting high. I had no kind of understanding about why I was doing all this.

"I look at my life hard, but I'm glad I learned the lessons that I learned. I'm sorry I was in my addiction for so long, but it is what it is. It happened, and I made it out the other side. I still see people around here that I used to get high with and I have my moments and then I think if I go back, I won't come back. If I start getting high and drinking again, I won't stop."

Today, Debra lives in a nine-floor building at the Geddes Housing Development, which towers above Skiddy Park. Eight years clean, she moved there after living in several other subsidized apartments around town where familiar drug merchants tried to lure her back to her old lifestyle. Certainly, her housing development claims its own dealers, but they don't know about her old drug affairs and they leave her alone.

A slender woman of 55 years, she spends her days keeping up with family and chatting with workers in the office of her apartment complex. She has a ride share job and relies on disability checks and housing subsidies, and she has become as inured to the gunfire and knife fights that plague her neighborhood as she is to the temptation of drugs.

"When we lived in my last apartment, the way it's set up, when you hear gun shots we used to hit the floor," recalled Debra. "The lady who lived under me, they fired into her bedroom window and shattered it. They could have lifted their gun up a little higher and hit my bedroom window. When you heard shots, me and my husband hit the floor. You wasn't immune to it down there. When you heard it, you had to run or do something, but where I'm at now, I hear them and pick up the remote and I'm still watching TV."

10

✧ ✧ ✧

CRASHING

The election of Donald Trump hit Syracuse like a rogue snowstorm. The majority Democratic electorate in the city reliably marched to the polls on November 8 and voted against him, and the county and the state followed suit. But the nation shunned Syracuse's example, choosing the man who stirred up its fears and whose board games, TV shows, books, casinos, failed businesses, and suburban country clubs it had patronized. Many Syracusans cried, dashed off indignant and fretful posts on social media, or threatened to move to Canada, only a ninety-minute drive away.

Despite the Hillary Clinton email scandal, serious questions around the Clinton Foundation, and her apologies for her husband's sexual predations, Syracuse just seemed more at home with her. After all, she had come to New York to build her political career, serving one term in the US Senate, and seemed in alignment with the city's refugee story, embrace of Obamacare for its poor and under-employed, and legacy in the women's rights movement.

During the campaign, Trump had preached against Mexicans, legally and illegally here, as well as Muslims whatever their national origin, and few in the Republican Party establishment had checked him. With the GOP in control of both houses of Congress, immigration issues, including the question of refugee resettlement, would probably jet to the top of Washington's agenda.

In Syracuse, a busy and diverse economy had grown up around refugee resettlement: the new immigrants had opened businesses and tackled low-level service jobs that home-grown Syracusans were loath to fill, and dozens of white-collar professionals worked in the social service sector to help refugees find homes and jobs, learn English, and enroll in government assistance programs. The days of its booming manufacturing long in the past, refugee resettlement was now the city's signature endeavor. It could be proud when national news stories highlighted the city's generosity, which invoked its immigrant legacy and the promise on the Statue of Liberty's tablets.

Particularly impressive were refugees of Nepalese descent who were cast out of Bhutan in the 1990s and forced to live for years on end in camps in Nepal. In Syracuse, they dove into work and ardently saved their earnings to buy homes. The local newspaper estimated that eighty families had bought homes in the city after less than a decade in America. "They came with few material goods," the article noted, "but they brought a way of life that expects hard work and happiness at the same time. The Bhutanese who came to Syracuse morphed from a culture of farmers to factory workers and health-care aides without losing their tight-knit sense of community."[1]

On January 27, the new president terrorized families in the city and across the country when he signed an executive order halting the flow of refugees into the United States until after its review of immigration policies. That meant about 220 refugees cleared for resettlement in Syracuse would bide their time in massive relocation camps or their home nations as they waited for the Trump administration to make up its mind about them. To say the least, the order threw the local refugee community into chaos: families expecting the arrival of loved ones worried about the safety of sons and mothers and brothers while social service agencies cut staff as federal funding for refugee resettlement slowed to a trickle.

1. Marnie Eisenstadt, "From Mud Hut to $100,000 Home," *Post-Standard,* July 2, 2017.

The next day, hundreds of people from the area—city and suburbs—swarmed the local airport to protest the ban while voices from across local government and law enforcement reassured many newly arrived refugees that they were safe in Syracuse. Mosques, churches, and resettlement agencies threw open their doors to welcome people with questions about Trump's unpredictable course.

On University Hill, Neil Murphy shot an email to his teaching assistant, Reza, who's from Iran, reassuring him that nobody would snatch him from his lab. "He's the nicest guy you'd ever want to meet," said Murphy of his charge. "Very committed, great personality, really good with people. Just an extraordinary young man." The next day the student showed up to his professor's office in gratitude.

"Look at some of our most extraordinary scientists," continued Murphy. "Albert Einstein was a refugee. Edward Teller was a refugee. The list goes on and on and on and on. In many respects our innovation businesses are heavily influenced by refugees. Here at ESF we have about six hundred graduate students; I'd say a third of them are international students. They enrich who we are. We're a better institution because they're here. They expand the horizons of all of our students. I'm sure there are undergraduate students that Reza has helped as a TA that now would love to go to Iran and see some of the things he's talked to them about over a cup of coffee. Their fear of nuclear conflagration is probably sharply diminished by having met him."

While Murphy and other Syracusans soothed their foreign friends, the federal courts stalled Trump's order. But relief was temporary. Who knew the final outcome? In the midst of uncertainty, reassuring gestures appeared throughout the city. In addition to friendly profiles of refugees in the local newspaper, a local choir staged an immigration-themed concert and, on the eve of Ramadan, yard signs popped up everywhere wishing Muslims a happy holiday.

Justo Triana learned about Trump's election win from the radio. He, too, had expected Clinton to win, but he had also solemnly noted the Trump juggernaut. However, the real shock came on November 25, 2016, as he emptied a garbage can at Upstate Hospital. A friend told him Fidel Castro had died.

> I wasn't expecting that at all. I really have good memories about my childhood, playing in the streets, my friends who were very nice at school. And Castro was part of my environment. I was in first grade, which is when you learn how to write, the first letters, first words. And there was a visit from the upper branch of the education

department. It was a very nice guy, an old guy, and he went to my classroom and he told us, "Hey, we will test you. Do you know how to write 'Fidel'? OK . . . open your notebooks. It's F-I-D-E-L." And the next day they came with paper and asked, "OK . . . do you know how to write 'Fidel'? Write it." He was in every moment that you can imagine. I do remember sometimes I wanted to watch the cartoons and there was this crazy guy speaking on TV. He gave a speech of seven hours once! That's how big his ego was. He only cared about himself. When he took a microphone and he knew that the whole country was forced to watch him, he was hard to stop. If you spent seven hours looking at yourself in the mirror—combing or straightening your hair—it's the same. I was very pissed off that he gave his speeches, and I couldn't watch my cartoons.

The people are mourning him in Cuba because they were so used to his presence, his daily presence, in every aspect of the country, like the Stockholm Syndrome. I think that's part of the reaction you've seen in Cuba right now. I can tell you right now they are bringing his ashes from Havana back to Santiago, Cuba, to put them in a beautiful cemetery where Martí's remains are. I've been there, of course. They're organizing a lot of people along the roads who are waiting and waving but I can tell you most of that is fake. Remember, Cuba is a whole country in a play. They are controlled. I'm pretty sure that my son has been there lining up against his will. The school is controlling you. It is free for you to go to school, but it is a way of controlling you and it is a way of indoctrination.

That's why I'm here, because I don't want my son to spend more than thirty years wasting his life, acting against his will. That's really stupid. You have to pretend that you're another person and that you have other feelings. It's sad. But I can assure you that most of the people I know feel the same as I.

The only similarity I see between Trump and Castro is that Trump is very temperamental. And this great ego, too. That's the only two traits I can see. The circumstances are different. He doesn't have the whole country behind him. Fidel took over the country with the whole country fighting behind him because they were fighting another tyrant, Batista, who was a really bad guy who killed a lot of people. By that time there were maybe five million people and he had with him everyone because he was the one who freed the country, so it was the right thing to do. But there was a hidden agenda. He managed to deceive all these five million people. Now with Trump it's different. He only has less than half the country, so it will be hard for him to take over. He lost the popular vote.

While the last light of another day faded behind him, Justo folded his clothing in a small laundromat on a busy Syracuse boulevard. The headlights of passing automobiles streaked the building's plate-glass windows, revealing the lonely figure at work. In such quiet moments, Justo contemplated his wife and two children, still back in Cuba and still waiting to be cleared by an immigration process that was in all likelihood going to be gummed up by the Trump presidency.

In truth, at that moment Justo was about to crash. Worries over his family, hours spent studying for standardized tests for his graduate school applications, and the strain of three jobs had depleted him. He was losing hair due to stress, hadn't slept regularly for months, and noticed his English skills—so necessary for his teaching—slipping whenever he was tired. On lucky days, he grabbed a total of five or six hours of sleep here and there in between jobs. "It's not natural," he complained. "You're violating your circadian rhythm. Even if you had a full eight-hour sleep during the day, the human body is not designed for that. You're programmed by evolution, by thousands of years, to follow the sun."

Since he was trying to bring his family here under a normal visa program, Trump's refugee ban wasn't as worrisome to him as it was to some of his students who were refugees.

They were really stressed, really concerned and nervous. Some of them were waiting for their families, who were in the process of coming over. It was really hard. They didn't even want to talk about it. In my morning class, I have two women from Iraq who didn't say a word. I was the one who brought it up and we discussed it. They were just expectant, waiting for something. It was pretty sad. The effect on their relatives was worse because they could get killed waiting to come here. They were needing more time to understand what's going on and what the developments would be. It's pretty saddening.

I have mixed emotions about [the ban] because on one hand there's people who are trying to escape those disastrous situations. But on the other hand, you have also the Americans that are supporting Trump who wholeheartedly feel they have enough problems to keep taking people in. So I think that both sides have good reason. There's a lot of fear because of terrorism and it's understandable. For example, the guy who killed forty-nine people in the Pulse nightclub [in Orlando in 2016] was of Afghanistan parentage. He was born in the United States so he was an inside terrorist. The way the world is moving today is pretty anti-Muslim, in Europe and the United States, too. I would say that a ban is not the right thing. If you want you can screen even deeper, in a very organized manner, but a ban is too aggressive, too radical. It's radical Christians fighting radical Islam.

In Justo's mind, Trump's ban also grew out of his well-known suspicion of people who have come to America from south of the border.

There should be a way to end this problem with the undocumented immigrants because those guys they are working like crazy in the US, eleven-hour shifts on the farms. They have no health insurance, no protections. I know them personally. They've been doing that for twenty years on the farms. I do think there should be a path to citizenship for those guys. It's pretty unfair. I think the bad guys that get into trouble should be deported.

But many of the good guys have been here for many years, working like dogs without rights, without proper housing. And everybody knows it: Democrats, Republicans, the police, the farmers, the politicians. That's really something that should be addressed for the sake of the country, for protecting the country, and for protecting those people. They should have rights. Everything is about the market, about the economy. They are making things cheaper. If you made those guys citizens, then they would have rights. Then they would have entitlement to a minimum wage.

And what about Mayor Stephanie Miner's refusal to enforce federal immigration policy with regard to undocumented immigrants, holding Syracuse up as a sanctuary city?

I think that the sanctuary cities is not the right way because there's not a legal definition of a sanctuary city. What it's really defying is the law and people should comply with the law, starting with the people in charge. Some political parties label themselves as protectors of people. They are just playing to their base, but I don't think it's fine, the idea of sanctuary cities. I'm talking from the point of view of a lawyer, right? Laws should be fair. We should fix the laws, not label the city as a sanctuary city. It is true that there are many people who are undocumented who are committing crimes. How do you check on it, if you know nothing about their legal status, if they don't have any identification or evidence? It's not okay to deport people just because they're here. You let them come here and you let them stay here and use their labor. So, both are guilty.

Justo's commentary raises nagging questions about the role of immigrants in Syracuse. The city proudly points to its immigrant tradition, but that tradition was built on a booming economy. Today, new immigrants, whether documented or undocumented, move here to discover a poverty rate that persistently hovers around 30 percent (with a 47 percent poverty rate among children). Syracuse is the thirteenth-most-impoverished city in the nation, and it recently ranked among America's most economically stagnant cities, which means that there's little job growth and wages lag far behind the national average.[2] No wonder that many, like writer Alana Semuels in *The Atlantic*, gently point out the apparent absurdity of relocating poor immigrants to a poor city: "Syracuse is still trying to figure out how to find housing for refugees who can't afford much and how to ensure, in a region where jobs are hard to come by, that refugees don't fall into perpetual poverty."[3]

However, people like Semuels may not be accounting for certain possibilities. In a city with high discouraged worker rates, refugees are bolstering

2. Mark Weiner, "Syracuse Poverty Rate Now 13th Worst," *Post-Standard*, September 14, 2017.
3. Alana Semuels, "The Refugees Who Come Alone," posted November 12, 2015, https://www.theatlantic.com/business /archive/2015/11/the-refugees-who-come-alone/415491/.

the workforce and taking jobs that natives won't fill. Additionally, continued growth in the refugee population could help sustain demand for local goods and services and counter the continued exodus of people, another possible jolt to the economy. And who can predict what novel ideas will spring from the fertile minds of newcomers?

But, for now, anecdotal evidence suggests that some new refugees, once they understand the possibilities of America, move on to other destinations. Hence, the city becomes one station on an assembly line, building up the language and job skills and education levels of recent arrivals before they move on to fortify booming economies elsewhere in the country. Syracuse does the same for qualified students who come from around the nation and the world to earn degrees at local universities and colleges and then bounce back to richer regions at home and abroad. Bereft of a substantial tier in the economy that can provide healthy wages and long-term security to those who come to town, Syracuse's economy is the economy of preparation, dependent on federal and state funding, tuition dollars, and a certain degree of white-collar expertise to train people streaming through the region. Whether they arrive in an airplane cabin or a birthing room in a local hospital, many are destined to move on, providing a focus for the city's preparation economy but very little in the way of long-term economic growth.

11

✧ ✧ ✧

A GLITTERING
NIGHT

Perhaps a few new immigrants will find their way into law enforcement, if Syracuse ever comes up with the budget dollars to adequately staff its police force. The department must pay officers overtime because funds don't exist or haven't been released to bring on new recruits, which means certain tracts of the city aren't regularly patrolled and many victims of crimes such as burglary must wait hours for cops to show up, if they show up at all. Like Jessi Lyons, who waited weeks for police to address marauding teens in her neighborhood, Elise Baker on the South Side learned where she stands when police took six hours to arrive after she reported a break-in at her home.

On the way home from the flower shop with her son Brandon, they stopped to pick up an acquaintance who needed a ride to an auto parts store. Brandon dropped Elise at her house and continued on with the hitchhiker. Immediately, she noticed damage to the lock on her front door. Inside, the house was in pieces.

The biggest thing that they took was my son's money, two hundred dollars. He had been rolling quarters and had money on his stand. They took all of that. I been trying to tell him about doors, saying "Bran, make sure you lock both of the locks." He said, "You always think somebody's going to take something. Ain't nobody going to take nothing."

They got me too. I lost jewelry. They must have thought that I'm somebody that I'm not because of the store. They think I got materialistic stuff. I'm plain and simple. The only diamond I wear is my sister's. The only diamond that I'll buy is if somebody buys one for me. They took all my gold, broken pieces or chains my son bought me. And a cross that was sentimental. My nephew bought me a watch for Christmas and it had little diamonds around the face. It ain't no real diamonds. They stole that. They ransacked my room and all of the oils on my dresser fell down into the drawers and on my clothes. They didn't steal no TVs, no Play Stations, nothing like that. They must have had time.

While Brandon sped back to the house, he noticed seven police cars at a nearby intersection crowded around a black driver. This was at 6:38 p.m. At the same moment, Elise telephoned the police about the break-in, but nobody showed up to help her. "Imagine if that was a senior in that house and nobody who could check on her. I have people who can check on me. They didn't ask me if I was all right or anything like that. That became the biggest problem. The thief had stolen what he's going to steal. That's materialistic. But when you pay taxes, you should be looked at. That's what their duty is, to serve and protect. You can't come and at least check that I'm all right, but it takes seven police for one dude? Then over on Valley Drive in the church parking lot, a friend saw three police cars sitting in the corner, just chilling."

As the hours passed, Elise lobbed complaints and updates on her Facebook page, and she called a city councilor she knew who offered to get involved. "I don't need a favor," she replied. "I want them to come to me just like they would if it was somebody that they knew."

Sometime after midnight, the police wheeled up to her house.

I was still waiting because I didn't want to mess with the evidence because I saw finger prints. They didn't want to do no fingerprints. They sent a young lady that was pure wet behind the ears. I said, "They had to send somebody nice because I am so upset with you guys. I'm so upset that it's not funny. I'm glad they sent you because now I can't go off like I want to." And I've cooled down, too, because I had to wait six hours. At 9:00 I was ready to fight everybody. She said, "I just came on shift and didn't know anything about it." She was apologetic as far as words were concerned: "Miss, I'm sorry that it happened like this." Then she wanted to go straight to the case. Compassionate in her own way. She had to be new on the force, period.

Fired up, Elise spent the next day lodging complaints in the mayor's office and the police department. To this day, she has never heard word one from either of them. She even called a local television station to pitch her story, but the assignment editor balked. Then another channel featured a general report on burglary in Syracuse, two days after she was victimized.

I called them and said, "It's amazing that you're doing this because I was just burglarized and if nothing else check on the emergency calls and

where they stand in regards to arrival times."
"We'll let you know," they said. Ain't heard nothing. They said they'd let me know but they didn't
take my name, phone number. I said, "Miss, you
didn't take any information from me, so can you
please have someone call me if they do need
me?" That's lack of concern. Nobody can tell me
that if I was in another neighborhood, even within
the city, that I wouldn't have gotten an answer
quicker than I got.

Even the police told me that I should have said
somebody was still in the house. I said, "I don't
have to lie to you all to get you here. You should
come." I would have gotten a quicker response. I
don't want to lie.

I'm trying to make sure we get the same service
that everybody else do, and I'm angry that they did
not treat me as a human being at that time. I don't
know what they treated me as to be perfectly honest with you, but I know I didn't like it.

I'm not going to be afraid. I don't care what
neighborhood I live in. I don't care where I'm at
in my community. I don't care if you're a crack-
head, you a heroin addict, a thief, whatever. I'm
not going to be afraid in my neighborhood. I've
been here long enough to know that you're not
going to do certain things to me and think it's all
right. You know what I'm saying? You're not going
to do it to my seniors or the babies. I'll stand up

for that. It's not about what they stole from me no more. It's about depriving me of my own home and other people having to go through that, like seniors that don't deserve that. The police . . . I don't know what we can do to change that. As a people we have to change ourselves and form things in our community that protects us.

Elise's implication that the police won't protect her community, not to mention her long-standing belief that the police, not the Skiddy Park partiers, were responsible for the Father's Day violence, came from mistrust that dated back ten years to Brandon's fraught encounters with law enforcement. "Every time he drove from [his suburban job] at nighttime, over and over, the police would pull him over just because." The reasons varied with each stop, she claimed: his hood was open, a headlight burned out, he fit the profile of a kidnapper, he looked like he was going to harm himself. She was having none of it. He was a black man driving in the suburbs. Frequently, she witnessed other examples of unequal treatment by police hands.

Yesterday, there was a situation. The police pulled over a car in front of my house. A black man was driving [with a white passenger]. This is after I saw on the internet three policemen beating a black man, just punching him in the head and the only thing they had to do was put the cuffs on. I said, "I'm going to watch the situation. I want to see what happens." It was an older police officer there and a younger police officer. The younger police, you could tell didn't want to do all the stuff like this other police doing who's teaching him. So, my son and I are sitting in the car watching this. You see the one being more aggressive, and the black dude looks like he's as scared as I don't know what. So I said Brandon, "I'm getting out of the car. You stay here. Don't come nowhere near me." I went down to where the incident is taking place because I want to make sure things is going to go right. They patting the black guy down, so the police is going between his legs and patting him and he says, "Oooo." They got him by his sack, it looked like. And he's trying to get a response out of him. So the younger cop has his eyes raised. And he says, "Hi how are you doing." I say, "Fine. How are you?" So I watched it. You could see he was just scared. Now, it could have been a drug dealer. There was a white man in the car, too, so they got him out and patted him down. He didn't grab him by his testicles and say, "Oooo." He didn't do none of that.

He made the black dude take off his socks, and they didn't make the other one take his socks off.

[The police officer] went in his police car, and then they went into the back seat of his car and now I'm thinking they're going to plant something on him. But they didn't because I stayed right there. The black man got behind the wheel and they told him, "No, let the white guy drive."

I watch everything in my neighborhood now. I watch it because it's so wrong.

A few miles away, in a small coffee shop, Stefon Greene concurred, mostly.

I can't ever think of a time when I had a good experience with a police officer. The most upset I've ever been at a cop was one time when my mom was on a bender for a while. It had to be a weekend or something, and she was attempting to leave. But I wouldn't let her leave the house, so she called the police and the police officer came and I explained the situation to him. He was like, "I can't let you confine her in the house." I felt like he understood where I was coming from and in a sense he kind of cared. He was like, "Here's this kid. His mom's on drugs. He's trying to keep her in the house safe. But legally I can't keep her in the house and I can't let you keep her in the house." That had to be the maddest I've ever been at a cop but also the best experience I've ever had with a cop.

I don't take anything away from the cops because the inner city can be a dangerous place, especially with the type of drugs that are out now.
It's worse now than ten years ago with the type
of drugs that people are using. It's dangerous and
there are so many more guns in the streets than
there were before.

Two weeks later, Elise Baker's attentions had shifted
away from the burglary but remained no less focused on the community. She hurried to arrange
flowers for the funeral of a niece and worked with
her son to put in place an adult cabaret. Since the
315 Spring Dance Fest at Henninger High School,
almost a year before, Brandon had staged male
dance reviews for adoring women and an open mic
poetry and music night in a former shoe store. The
poetry slam had shone like patent leather, moving him to stage the cabaret in an obscure spot on
S. Salina Street that appeared from the outside to
be a defunct tire shop.

Inside, though, the place was crisply finished:
mauve-painted cinder-block walls, polished concrete floors, and aluminum duct work for a cool industrial look. Darting about the space in a tie-dyed
blouse, Elise sanded down the hard edges, lighting
candles that reflected softly on bottles of wine and

setting up cocktail tables for that Copacabana feel. On the bar, she had spread out trays of mouthwatering pasta and salads. There was no liquor for sale, however. That had come in the door tucked away in handbags and coat pockets.

While Elise guided guests to tables and scooped up dirty dishes, Brandon collected tickets and coached the emcee, Jamel Lorick, a.k.a. "Mr R&B Singer," whose glittery blazer Brandon had designed and decorated himself. Lorick was more than equipped to carry the night. Wooing middle-aged women with grinding versions of Al Green standards, he also introduced each of the amateur dancers, poets, gospel singers, and urban crooners, who were backed by a versatile house band. A tree of lamps, like what you'd see next to a couch in a college apartment, cast a subtle light on the bandstand.

In a nod to Elise's emphasis on community, Brandon, who would rap a little later, introduced a neighbor who's battling cancer. She told her story, pointing out that until recently, she was in remission. Now, the cancer was back. "But I'm still here," the woman proclaimed. "God be the glory," replied Elise. She was followed by a krump dancer, a bashful poet, and a young woman who sang like Whitney Houston. It became a night of poets and politicians when mayoral candidate Alfonso Davis took the stage, imploring the crowd to vote for him in the late summer Democratic primary. He complimented Brandon for hosting a positive experience for the community—there are so few available—but then he admonished the crowd for staying home from the polls even when black politicians like him are running for citywide office. "We choose not to engage. No one can silence your voice but you. There are 14,000 registered voters who look like you, but we don't engage." And who's to blame for the South Side's economic woes? Apparently, to some extent, the black people in front of him, whom he scolded for going outside the community to shop and for asking Elise for discounts when they buy flowers.

Later, Elise confided that she lost money on the evening, but like the Spring Dance Fest, she had provided a showcase for black talent, a safe destination for a community starved for classy entertainment, and an alternate narrative to the crime-drugs-violence story that defines the South Side in the eyes of many. If only more Syracusans had witnessed the stage she set. "Hope was served," she wrote in a text after the event.

When mayoral candidate Davis retreated into the audience after his comments, a gospel singer named Carla D. Mason belted out an exuberant testimony to God's power and grace. As if on cue, as Mason reached her first crescendo, Elise walked to the cancer patient and hugged her until the music stopped.

12

✧ ✧ ✧

THE TRIAL

The main hallway in downtown's new criminal justice building runs straight into a tall glass wall where lawyers, defendants, families of the accused, and reporters gather. Talking on their cellphones or absent-mindedly sipping from a soda cup during a recess from the courtroom, they observe the meeting of sky and cityscape, the scene of assaults, drug deals, and muggings that may be resolved in this very building. The view from the hallway invites reflection, no doubt, while the natural light transmits energy for a full afternoon of proceedings.

In January of 2017, in the chambers of Judge Thomas J. Miller, all minds focused on Skiddy Park. Six men who converged on the Father's Day picnic back in June stood accused of inciting a riot. Clad in suits, plaid shirts, and hoodies, they sat, each next to his attorney, behind a long L-shaped table, warily following the arguments and testimony. Except for one forty-year-old elder statesman, the defendants—on trial as one—had barely reached drinking age.

From their wooden chairs, the accused watched video of their actions during the Skiddy Park melee, culled by police from a host of social media accounts, including the men's own Facebook pages, used to formulate a damning case against them. It portrayed, at worst, a breakdown of human civility or, at best, the party-goers' savvy use of new technology in the post-Ferguson era to record police as they collected evidence and searched for Officer Kelsey Francemone's attackers.

On a small screen that delivered everybody to the tragic evening in 2016, the courtroom audience could see the defendants in front of yellow tape where police formed a line to protect the crime scene. Men and women taunted the cops, volleyed obscenities, threatened violence, and hurled projectiles scavenged from the ground. The eldest defendant, Jamie Crawford, held his camera high and assured his accomplices that as long as he was recording they could do whatever they wanted without fear of reprisal. And then he urged an officer to throw something back that had been thrown at him. A hidden female voice interjected, "Throw it, and I'll put it on Snapchat."

In the picture, Crawford turned to an uneasy black officer at the front of the line. "You the face of white oppression . . . and your skin is darker than mine," he charged. The police officer merely stared forward, beyond his detractors, to an easier day, perhaps.

At about the same time, the video revealed Police Chief Frank Fowler rolling into the area. He'd been rousted from his Father's Day night by the shift commander reporting the attack on Francemone. Within minutes, he was in the defendant's cellphone shot, fresh meat for the jeerers who crowed about Fowler's son, who has a long criminal history. And then more objects rained down. The chief ordered his officers to uncap their mace, which shut down the defendant and his followers. "You faggot-ass niggers," hollered the defendant as the crowd dispersed and the screen went dark.

It didn't look good for Crawford in the courtroom. Who could deny that he had tried to bait the blue line behind the yellow tape? The jury—which included two women of color—stared grimly at the video, wincing at the coarse language Crawford and his friends lashed their adversaries with.

In a setting where every sight in the courtroom was on trial—the neckties of the defendants, the ruddy face of a defense lawyer, the sleek suit of a man with the prosecution who frequently whispered to the people's lead attorney—Crawford's digital performance was a flop. His mumbled apologies and claims of innocent stupidity floated unnoticed toward the white ceiling. The white bailiffs, white lawyers, white prosecutors, white court reporter, white walls, and white judge seemed unimpressed.

After Crawford eased back in his chair behind the long table, codefendant Luis Reyes took the stand with the starry-eyed anticipation of a television game show contestant. He, too, had shot video and posted it for the world to see. "That's what we do these days," the twenty-three-year-old told the court.

On Father's Day, Reyes had used his day off from a tile company to rip through the city on his motorcycle and then had veered toward Skiddy Park when news of the cookout popped up on his Facebook newsfeed. Before the charcoal had begun to glow, the cellphone-obsessed biker had joined the party.

In the courtroom gallery, Reyes's mother shifted on the slippery bench, anxious for the truth to be known. "He was drunk," she hissed, within earshot of all the observers. "Just say it." Indeed, Reyes needed some kind of defense because his video was as self-incriminating as Crawford's. The images pulsing on the screen in front of the court surveyed the Skiddy Park chaos: an officer trying to arrest a woman, small groups of locals dashing across the green, and a crowd of people gathering around

Kelsey Francemone just after she had shot Gary Porter. In the audio, the court could hear Reyes call out, "Why did you shoot the man? The homeboy's dead."

He continued to harass her as she attempted to render aid. Then, as the crowd around her closed in, Reyes demanded her badge number. But she remained focused on Porter. Which only incited Reyes. "I'll fucking knock you out!"

Then the crowd swarmed over her.

In the gallery, the mother stiffened. "He was drunk out of his mind."

Days later, the jury delivered a "not guilty" verdict. As scurrilous as the six defendants' words had sounded, members decided there was no evidence that they incited the rioting on that night in June. In other words, their epithets, taunts, and threats had not stretched beyond the First Amendment's protection.

Little was ever spoken again in Syracuse about that Father's Day night. Police–community mediators disappeared and new violence replaced the old violence. Wayward men and women continued to post their after-dark misadventures on social media while police and people in some neighborhoods observed an awkward truce. Predictably, there was no end in sight to illegal gun ownership and the drug trade. Like most sores in Syracuse, they remained bandaged. Never healed.

While the six men ambled away from the court-house, suit jackets fluttering against the stern breeze, Justo Triana continued his lectures in a classroom little more than two miles away. His mornings teaching English in a public school program for immigrants and evenings teaching refugees for a non-profit agency, all before sweeping floors over-night at the hospital, had chipped away at his focus and energy. At night, he squirmed in bed, wired by intense studying for the GRE and TOEFL exams. Trump's unwelcome election and whether or not it would thwart his and his family's application for citizenship distracted him, too. At that moment, he had no time to practice his guitar or meet friends socially.

But the refugee families he saw pouring into the drab school building on the North Side in the eve-nings encouraged him. In the classroom, he dashed around seeking examples to demonstrate words and phrases that earlier he had impeccably noted on the worn chalkboard. To illustrate the meaning of the word "expensive," he held up his gold wed-ding band as his eyes darted around the classroom. Then, spying a plastic bottle, he ingeniously tore the perforated ring from its neck and placed it on his finger to illustrate the word's antonym: "cheap."

Maintaining his taut pace, he induced little dramas in the class, teasing a married couple, hiding a notebook from its distracted owner. These moments led to conversations in which students pulled from their previous English lessons. And when Somali women and Nepalese friends remembered correctly, modest smiles appeared on their faces.

At the break, a jubilant parade of refugee children rolled from their educational playgroups dressed in the world's every color. They spun around the hallways, peeking their eager faces into the classroom to check on their parents. Burkas made of shiny fabric reflected the ceiling lights' drab glow while lovely sandals, which would provide little protection from the coming winter snow, slid across the bare floors, raising up dust and a grainy shuffle beat.

It was another scene—like the Spring Dance Fest that Elise Baker hosted—that most middle-class Syracusans never see. If they did, maybe the city would open its arms even wider for the new residents. And if only Donald Trump and Steve Bannon could visit this place, they might discern the future of America.

The break almost over, while Justo waited for the seats to fill up again, a Vietnamese woman asked him about Trump. "No matter who's running the country," he told his student, "we have to move forward."

A few days later, the teacher reflected on his classroom:

> It's beautiful to be there. These guys are so nice. They are salt of the earth people. They are so naïve. You have to get to know them in order to love them. It is hard because most American people don't interact with these guys. For example, it's not only the classroom . . . at the hospital, most of my co-workers are immigrants. I have a friend from Bosnia, there are more Cubans and Africans and Muslims from the Middle East, people from the Ukraine. Most of them are very hard workers and nice people and we really enjoy the company with each other. It is really fun. I'm surrounded by immigrants all the time: in the morning, in the evening, in the night.
>
> But many are not interacting with native-born Americans. If you don't interact with others, they cannot know how you are. It is a normal culture clash. When the Italian wave and the German wave of a hundred years ago happened, it was the same thing. The first-generation immigrants rarely interact with people, unless you have a very good acquaintance with the language or with the culture. If you are a high-skilled worker you are more able to interact with people to get along with

Americans, but otherwise you don't have that opportunity. It will be your children who will be fully American, and that's what's happening. It takes a generation.

There is one thing that's very important to keep in mind . . . the Italians and Germans who immigrated, they were very concerned with assimilation into American culture. Even one of my first ESL teachers came from Lebanon and her parents were very strict about not teaching her Arabic because their main target was to assimilate as far as they can to English, to American culture, to become Americans right off the bat. That's very different from immigration now. People from other countries, especially from Middle Eastern countries, are not vowing to assimilate to take the best of this culture. That's what I see. Maybe they are isolated by the society, but maybe they're isolating themselves, too. When you have isolation and poverty together, you have stabbings and shootings and radicalization.

Those of us from Latin nations have to tinker some things but mainly, in my case, I haven't had to adjust to a lot of things, just getting acquainted with the language, and that's it. Maybe some cultural tips, like themes of conversations, that's it. It hasn't been a big deal. I know, for example, I'm atheist. It's different. Maybe if I were a Muslim it would be harder.

In order to let people know you, you have to
break that isolation. It's hard. When they come
here, they don't have any place to go to practice
the language. They only have their friends and
families, so it's a vicious circle. For example, I
know that many Americans, in good faith, cannot understand why a woman has to wear a hijab
or why they can't drive or why they can't speak.
Why they have to be so submissive. But it's a normal clash of cultures and I hope that things play
out well. But I'm not so sure that will happen. So
far, what has happened in France and Belgium,
we see Muslim communities living completely isolated. It feels like a city within a city. There are
Muslim neighborhoods completely isolated with
their own culture and languages. We have to work
on it. Maybe I think it shouldn't be just bringing
people here. That's not the point. You have to
bring people, but only if you have an infrastructure
ready to assimilate them, to prepare them. If you
bring an immigrant here from whatever place in
the world and after four or six months you don't
send them to school or if you only give them six
months of schooling and then he just has to get a
job, it is hard to assimilate them.

In my class, women from Burma and Somalia
sit next to each other. The Burmese woman was
touching the hijab of the Somali woman, curious
about her hair. They were touching each other.

They were happy. I was so happy looking at it. It was happening unconsciously. They are the things that need to happen here. We need people to get to know each other, not to fear each other. Because most of this anti-immigration sentiment and most of these radicalized killings come especially from not knowing each other.

After class, there was talk of going for a beer. But Justo refused. He had to be at University Hospital in a few hours to clean bathrooms. As it stood, he'd only eke out two or three hours of sleep. Besides, he won't take chances with drinking and driving. It could hurt his chances for citizenship. And his family's.

13

✧ ✧ ✧

BURNING DOWN

Dark clouds churned above Syracuse University in April of 2017 while hundreds of locals jammed into an ornate lecture hall for a much-touted debate over city-county consolidation. College students in knit caps and white-haired seniors wrapped in thick sweaters filled every seat and sat in the narrow aisles while deep in the well of the room the debaters bobbed and shuffled in anticipation of their task ahead. If people had still smoked indoors, a vapory blanket hugging the ceiling would have completed the picture.

Each side put forth two formidable competitors: Mayor Stephanie Miner and County Comptroller Bob Antonacci on the "no" side versus former congressman James Walsh and Bill Byrne on the "yes." But the absence of County Executive Joanie Mahoney on the affirmative side was a disappointment. Her beef with Miner had become so mythic that to see her sitting ringside was like showing up to the Thrilla in Manila only to learn that Joe Frazier was watching from the third row.

The Consensus Commission's final report, released in February of 2017, had seized local headlines by advocating for one metropolitan government to replace the city and county governments. According to the implementation plan, a new legislature would emerge, representing all county residents, including five districts exclusively for the city and nine districts that straddled the city and county, addressing fears over disenfranchisement in the city and encouraging cooperation with the shared jurisdictions. The rest of the county would be divided into fifteen districts. Always wary of the meddling hands of politicians, the commission called on geographers to create the legislative districts.[1] Although a host of other proposals filled the report, the "one government" idea incited politicians across the area and promised to dominate the evening bout.

1. The Consensus Commission's final report: the report is available at https://www.cgr.org/consensuscny/docs/Final Report-COMMISSION-FORMAT.pdf.

When the bell rang, Byrne stood at the podium with the familiar list of arguments. Consolidation would save money, eliminate duplicative services, and turn around the region's dismal economy. The president of the region's best-known dairy company, Byrne was the only contestant that night who had never held political office. And it showed. His argument, admirably rooted in logic, was about to be punched in the stomach.

As if the Stephanie Miner who vacantly addressed Skiddy Park mourners almost a year before had never existed, the mayor came out swinging with pointed appeals to the crowd's loyalty. Syracuse protected refugees, gays, minimum-wage workers, and impoverished students who couldn't afford to go to college, she argued, suggesting that consolidation would absorb the city's disenfranchised into a suburban sponge of indifference. Furthermore, she said without notes, or evidence, current city residents could expect no municipal trash pickup and poor firefighting services.

Equal to her in stature, former congressman Walsh replied that even Miner had to admit that resources were few and the city was reeling. During her tenure, she had closed a firehouse, cut staffing, and curtailed road improvement. That sent red splotches creeping up Miner's neck while Walsh and Byrne further argued that the city was heading for bankruptcy. Only a major rethinking of regional government could save it.

But the night belonged to Miner. In response to Walsh and Byrne's uninspiring argument, she pounded away at the idea that consolidation would lead to abandonment of the city people, including its schools. We have seen "magical solutions" before—referring to the bloated hopes around big malls and state-funded development projects. "But the revenue has never met the promises."

Then she unpeeled a sloganized conclusion: "Nothing is free!" "Truth isn't in a press conference!" "The city is the ultimate American experiment!" And she curiously harked back to advice she once received that to solve poverty cities had to integrate schools and housing, two areas that remained untouched by her mayoralty, not to mention Consensus. As if on cue, a woman stood among the audience and prophesied that until the community deals with racism and socioeconomic problems, no student on the South Side would get an education equal to his or her fellow citizens in the eastern suburbs. Down in the well, the debaters sat blankly.

When the evening began, attendees had cast ballots on the Consensus plan, a sort of pre-test before the debate, and the "yeas" had won. But after the match, after Miner's searing performance, the crowd had changed its mind. The majority voted "no," and then they clutched their purses or the arms of the ones who brought them and dashed into a spitting rain.

Neil Murphy watched the debate on a live stream in his home not two miles away from the confrontation. Perhaps he couldn't stomach being there, his animosity toward Stephanie Miner at an all-time high. Indeed, some weeks later, he still fumed over the mayor, especially her claim to be protector of the disenfranchised.

> The mayor took a page out of Trump's book in the debate with Hillary Clinton, coming up and almost getting right in their faces. I have no respect for either one of them [Antonacci and Miner] and what they say to me is absolutely immaterial because they haven't said anything of substance. I think I told you before that I met with the mayor twice, just me and she the only people in the room. And I asked her the question, "Mayor, if you don't like it, what do you like?" And neither time did I get an answer to the question. The second time, the only response was "Neil, politics are messy." Neither one of them is interested in the people of this county and this city. They're interested in themselves.

If they are taking care of people, how come we have the highest unemployment rate among minority groups of any city of our size in the US? We were not ranked that way before she took office. Brookings had us ranked at 96th out of 100 cities of our size in terms of economic stagnation.[2] We were not ranked that way years ago. In my opinion she has done nothing to improve the lives of those people who need help. She talks about it a lot. Look at Syracuse Housing Authority. How many employees does Syracuse Housing Authority have? It's around 125. Syracuse Housing Authority's primary function is to improve housing for all of the people in the city of Syracuse. If you were to look at it, I think you would find that the majority of those people are political hacks that she's brought on to the payroll because she can't hire them through civil service. Her premise as far as being the protector who will protect against the looting of assets of the city is just pure BS.

The last vehicle I got was a pickup truck and because I have to drive the city streets a lot because I live in the city, all I can tell you is that I'm very glad I picked a pickup truck because the city streets are in such horrible shape. You know how many miles they've programmed in the budget

2. In rankings of cities according to economic activity, Brookings placed Syracuse at 95th in 2016 and 100th in 2017.

for road repair? I think it's two miles to be resurfaced and there are 440 miles in the city. It would take us 200 years to resurface all the streets in the city. Two water main breaks a week on the average in the city of Syracuse. And yet the Syracuse water department makes money. They make about 2.5 million dollars a year. Where does that money go? It doesn't go back into the water infrastructure. It goes into the general operating funds of the city.

In other words, complained Murphy, if anybody is looting assets, it's the city itself, robbing profits from one service to subsidize others. He blanched also at the oft-quoted argument by Antonacci that state taxes and mandates are the real problems plaguing the county and other counties around the state.

It's insane. We spend—all thirty-six units of government in the county—1.7 billion dollars a year, and there's not efficiencies that can be wrought out of that 1.7 billion a year? Does Albany send Medicaid expenses to the county and the city, the answer is yes. But it has nothing to do with a mandate out of Albany. If you look at Antonacci, what was the result of him filing a lawsuit against the county executive [over salary increases], total amount of salary increase was fifty-eight thousand dollars.

What was the result of that? Three hundred and fifty thousand dollars spent on legal expenses.

One option for consolidated government is to expand the city limits to the current limits of the county and have it be Metropolitan Syracuse. If that is done, what has the city lost? I can't think of one damn thing the city will have lost. We could have the ability through efficiencies to deliver other services to the inner core of our Metropolitan Syracuse. Miner referred to the ideas we produced as looting the city's assets. Tell me what asset would be looted out of the city? Are we taking swings out of a park? Are we going to take water away from the residents of the city? What are we looting? Not a single asset would be taken out of the inner core of this new metropolitan community.

If my house is burning down, I want my house to be in the city of Syracuse. I don't want my house to be in Liverpool, I don't want my house to be in Marcellus. I don't want my house to be in Manlius or Dewitt. Now, they may have Taj Mahals for their fire departments where they spend millions of dollars for a new building, but they simply cannot respond the way the city fire department can respond. The city fire department is an ISO Class 1 fire department.[3] It's the highest class

---

3. Insurance Services Office is a not-for-profit organization that rates the quality of a department's fire protection.

you can get in terms of fire-fighting proficiency. The captains who are on the vols—Fayetteville, Manlius—they say, "Our over-the-road gear is so complex that we can't fundamentally train them the way they should be trained. We want the city to train our people." Somebody's got to go a long ways to tell me there aren't services in the city that are provided better than the suburbs. There is EMS coverage in the far reaches of the county that we said are not adequate coverage. Frankly, they need better coverage in some of those areas. It's not just poor services in the city and much better services in the suburbs. You have to look at each service and how it's being provided, how effectively it is being provided. You have to look at each one.

Murphy shook the ice in his empty paper cup and grimaced. A blue sky was visible through the window of his office.

Three years before, a village mayor had called Murphy into his office and offered cooperation on the Consensus endeavors, and Stephanie Miner had sent the commission a letter of support. But those days seemed long ago. "There's some incredible people in this community," he observed quietly.

I think there are people who believe that they have a responsibility to help and participate to lift the community up. I've met some really good politicians. Politicians who were very honest, very open and committed. And yet I've seen the other side of things, too, where there is a little too much self-focus, not enough sense of responsibility for others that can't necessarily fend for themselves. I've learned some good things and I've learned some things that have surprised me about the community. Not the people so much in the community but the institutions in the community. I don't blame anybody who would say that they don't support Consensus because of fear. It just shows that the knowledge level isn't where it needs to be and the trust isn't where it needs to be. What I do have a problem with is those people who are against it, but they won't even say why they're against it and they won't work and engage themselves and come up with something that they think could work better. I could care less whether what's in our final report is fundamentally adopted as long as the content of that report provided the catalyst to do something.

But what concerns me is that we're down to eighteen million dollars in the city in reserves, something like that. This year we consumed twelve million [from those reserves] to balance the budget. If we wait for a fiscal control board to run the city, I don't think it's going to be a very nice place to live in. I think we have the time to decide what we as a community want to do, so we don't have to rely on a fiscal control board to decide what they are going to do. I can't help but think about Flint, Michigan. I can't help but think about an administrator that made a decision for the sake of two hundred dollars a day—round numbers—that an anti-corrosion agent wouldn't be added to the drinking water. For the sake of two hundred dollars a day. There was human suffering as a result of that decision.

I have a lot of faith in all of the water professionals in the county. We have some extraordinarily good people who would never, ever, ever allow that to happen. Why should we ever put them in a position where they have to take the direction from an appointed administrator simply because we weren't able to manage our own resources? That would be a tragedy.

After a year managing the Brady Farm, the basic task of planting and harvesting fields of vegetables achieved, Jessi's other goals for the urban farm came back into focus, including the need to find employees who could carry the farm into the future. So while she still envisioned the broad goals of a Syracuse food economy growing up around local produce, she reassessed the farm's immediate next steps.

Are we really ready to jump forward with a barn, for example. But if I'm not really doing the hard work of putting people in a position to give leadership in those decisions and help me to make those things happen, am I doing my job? If we get a barn, so what? Am I really going to be able to use it in the most meaningful way. So maybe that's not a great use of seventy thousand dollars, or whatever it's going to take to build a barn, so I've slowed down my thinking.

There's the challenge of hiring people to harvest vegetables who don't eat vegetables, like the time all of my eggplant got picked regardless of ripeness. The picker had never eaten eggplant and didn't really care. I really need to be able to give time to training people and developing their relationship with food.

It was Terrence who doesn't care about vegetables. He said to me, when we were talking about getting food for something, "Why don't we just get donuts?" I said, "Not all food is good for you. Some of it's kind of poison and that's a kind of poison to the body." He said, "No, food is food is food. Let's do it." But then he talks to me, "I want people to eat healthier." This is a week later. His family has access to all of this produce and he brought home broccoli twice and that's pretty much it. They won't eat vegetables. He's this great case study. But he's also like, "Here's how you

hawk vegetables." He's sold more vegetables out
of his backpack than I was able to sell at our farm
stand. And that's him going up to guys and saying, "Hey . . . you got to buy your girl vegetables."
He was successful at that. It didn't matter that he
didn't really care about the vegetables, but he'd
got this marketing sense about things that's very
effective.

Someday, figured Jessi, Terrence would be an ideal
farm manager, but until he improved his communication skills and a few other things, she had to find
another candidate.

I've got a lot of pushback because I'm mostly hiring white people. I don't have a lot of people of
color stepping up who have the skills. Most of the
people who are interested in this type of work
who have these kinds of skills no longer live here.
They have left. They are doing better things with
their lives right now if they have the skills and experience that I need for this position. They have
moved on. There's some tension between employing people from the community and giving them
skills while mostly hiring white people in leadership positions. I have to hire people that I need
so that I can get people like Terrence where they
need to be, recognizing that I can't give him attention and the other people attention and make the

farm work and keep it funded. I need somebody
to come to the table with skills.

But at least Terrence takes ownership of the
farm. I asked him where he'd like to live in the
city and he said, "Next to the farm so I can take
care of it." He is a farmer. But I can't turn over
the keys to him, I can't give him that because he's
not qualified yet. So I want him to have the skills
and the decision making tools to be able to trust
him. I want him to be there. I don't want him to
move on. He's a musician and he's a poet and he's
really passionate about the creative arts. He wants
to have a business. Long term I want him to have
a sense of how to move forward.

Two miles away, on a ridge in the city that over-
looks the Brady Farm's neighborhood, Trevor Russell was coaching his own new employee. Trevor
had left the property management company on the
North Side for a job with a landlord who owns various properties throughout the city. His new boss, an
Italian native, had hired several immigrants from
places like Myanmar, Guatemala, and Syria and
assigned them to Trevor, a natural-born teacher if
there ever was one.

A young Pakistani man named Imam followed
him step by step, noting how his mentor repaired

leaky roofs and installed new siding. Soon, he was helping on the job and joining in the teasing and cutting contests around the workplace.

A few weeks into his apprenticeship, Imam showed up alone at one of the boss's apartment buildings and hoisted a ladder up to the roof to install shingles. An employee in the management office dashed out to stop him. She ran back in the building and called Trevor. Was this guy ready to shingle? "You bet," he answered.

Back at home, ever the public character, Trevor similarly nurtured kids on the block. Small children learned to properly walk his dog and, in the late summer, pick tomatoes with the right touch and at precisely the right time. Teenagers earned a few bucks helping Sheetrock his dining room or gathering up refuse from a nearby roof job done on the side. And still he was the protector, the guy you wanted on the front lines.

Trevor's heroics in the altercation in the alley had become part of neighborhood folklore when, two months later, another eye-popping confrontation sealed his legend. As he edged his truck up to a four-way intersection on the street where he and his people lived, a red sedan screamed through the stop sign and cut him off. Trevor merely shrugged in a "what-the-hell" kind of way, just another discourteous moment in a day in the life of a city dweller. He thought nothing of it, until he pulled from the intersection and noticed the red car stopped in front of him.

Perplexed, Trevor inched around the vehicle and continued down the street, making sure not to stop at his house lest the offending driver see where he lived. He circled around the block, through the same intersection, only to find the car parked in the same place. Again, Trevor approached. Only this time, like a scene of reckoning in a hot rod movie, he stopped and bellowed through the open windows. "Nice move."

In a flash, the driver, a stranger to the street, charged from the car and punched Trevor square in the face. A passenger emerged, pulling the attacker back. And then the car sped away. But not before the bruised survivor snapped a photo of the license plate for the police.

It was of no use. A police officer located the car at an address outside the city, but he seemed only vaguely interested in following up. "Isn't this assault?" Trevor asked the cop. There was a promise to get back in touch, but he never heard from him again. Nor did he again see the driver, who apparently resolved to steer clear of the block-long strip of Trevor's turf.

14

✧ ✧ ✧

REDEMPTION

While Neil Murphy wrestled with the Consensus opponents and Trevor Russell nursed his bruised face, Stefon Greene dealt with an unsettling new environment at work. In the two years since hiring on at the television station, he had received praise for his work shooting video and editing and producing a program on healthy lifestyles, and he had worked with a committee on morale-boosting initiatives, such as special pre-screenings of new TV shows for employees and cubicle name tags so people could get to know each other. But a new producer recently had arrived from Hollywood, a veteran of big productions, and she was churning the young man's stomach.

According to Stefon, she suggested he go back to his part-time jobs—in grocery stores and restaurants—while he sharpened his skills with freelance bones that she might throw his way. She told him he failed to emphasize to guests he booked for public affairs shows how grateful they should be for the exposure, and she bragged about engineering the terminations of people who had gone over her head in other jobs lest he think about doing the same. Later, she twisted the knife again, claiming that he'd spent his whole life just getting by—in school, on the job.

Like many people his age, Stefon unwisely took his problems to Facebook, grousing that about the unpleasant vibes at work. Said Stefon later, "She calls me and says sarcastically, 'I just want to make sure you feel appreciated.' As I feel more and more uncomfortable being there, I just feel like it's not conducive to my progress and my career. I'm getting to the point where I just agree and go along with it. And I go to work, and I smile and I laugh and I act like I'm happy when I'm not. And I feel bad about taking my stress home. Naureen clearly sees it when I'm upset, and I have a bad day.

"It got to the point where [the producer] said she was putting me on probation. After a month went by, I was never officially notified, so I went to the HR representative and I told her what happened." It turned out the producer had never instituted probation nor an accompanying improvement plan.

Her threats, it appeared, were just another round in the mind games that she was playing. "I don't want to think that people in the industry are like that, but maybe people in Hollywood are like that. Maybe the industry is like that, and she's the tip of the iceberg."

Increasingly, people in high positions called on him to be an in-house racial compass. Is this brochure racially sensitive? Is that promo sufficiently diverse? He squirmed. But he played along, like when a senior staffer asked him to look at remarks that an executive was making to a majority-black audience. "I was honest with her. I said, 'You're having a racial discussion about people that uses the term "diversity" too much. Why? You're expressing the fact that you want to build diversity, but you're telling people in a forum that they're different. That's how it would come across to me, if I were sitting in that forum.' She thanked me and later told me not to tell anybody that I had helped her."

Another employee asked Stefon to take a look at a community-oriented video spot that showed black children from the city riding horses in the country. He thought it was racist.

"She said, 'Why do you think that's racist?' 'Because I'm a black kid from the city! Black kids who live in the city don't normally do things like that. When you frame an urban kid in the country you're giving him access to something he normally doesn't

have access to. You're reminding him of his disad-
vantages.' And that's how I felt."

When his corner of the station became too dark
to bear, he forced his mind back to the hard times
and temptations he'd overcome.

In high school, my guidance counselor said, "You
should just drop out and get your GED. It would be
easier at this point." I was leaving eleventh grade
with a quarter of the credits I was supposed to
have. But I took fifteen courses in my senior year
and I graduated. But I was still thinking, "Maybe
if I sell weed I can make a little extra money over
the summer." And I was still partying too much.
Even at community college I still wasn't all the
way attached to what I wanted to do. We were living in Pioneer Homes, and I still knew everybody
around there, so selling drugs was still a pull. My
first major was hospitality management. I was just
coming from a restaurant job and thinking I could
open a club or something in that realm. I said,
"There's money in alcohol. People want to drink
and dance. I want to be a restaurateur." But things
change. I learned that people go to college to realize what they want to do and things like that. And
I was lucky enough to know that I wanted to tell
stories, so it was kind of a natural progression.

It still was hard not doing those things that
were fun for me, like hanging out with my friends

who were still in that world and sold drugs and stuff like that. I couldn't take the chance of being in a car with them and being arrested or going to a club in Syracuse where something bad could happen. God forbid, I could get shot. I have all these responsibilities now, so I shelter myself more. I stay in a little bit more. I don't do as much. I watch more TV and things like that. And put myself outside of it. It's caused issues between me and Naureen. She's fun and outgoing, and she loves to dance. She loves to go to the club, and she loves to go out. I do when I can.

I've known some smart young men that have not wanted to do work and have just taken the easy way out. But for me selling drugs wasn't the easy way out. It was difficult. I didn't like the stress, and I didn't like the long nights. It was the same thing when I didn't want to be the line cook because I didn't like the stress, and I didn't like the drinking and the partying that was part of the restaurant life. And I just didn't like that about selling drugs. I didn't like the fast-paced lifestyle. I had to realize that I wasn't good at it. I wasn't making a ton of money either. The people I was buying drugs from was making a lot of money because they weren't selling drugs to the people using drugs. They were selling drugs to the people who are selling drugs, and that far down the ladder you're not making money. I had to tell myself that. It was a conscious decision that I wanted to be something different and I had to accept the fact that it's going to be harder and I have to go to school and I have to pay attention and do those things and really give it my all. So when the TV station gives me the feeling that I've just been getting by, that's discouraging. That's disheartening.

But when I take a chance in my job or do freelance projects, it always reminds me of why I want to do this job in the first place. I could have the worst day at the station but then the next day do an on-camera interview with somebody that reminds me why I want to do this. I think that's what keeps me going. I know I'm happy doing this. A lot of this was the glamour of going to work in TV two years ago, the vastness of the studio, the newness of the building and feeling like I'm working toward something. A lot of that has gone away. But it still bubbles up a little every once in a while.

Stefon's troubles at the station directly influenced his questions about whether or not to remain in Syracuse or leave the city for another job, a place like Atlanta where a few of his relatives live and thrive. Little did he know that Neil Murphy's mind was tuned to that very same Peach State metropolis, not as a retirement destination but because his youngest daughter had moved there in 2015 with her husband and their daughter and he missed them terribly.

Recently, the young family had visited Syracuse, but they showed no signs of moving back. "There was a discussion over wine and beer," explained Murphy. "I was secondary to it but I heard my son and my son-in-law talking. 'When are you going to come back?' He said, 'There's no opportunity here.' Now I absolutely disagree with that. So I personally have experienced it. Every time they leave to go back to Atlanta, I start crying. One of the things that resonated in the Consensus presentations that I've made was this issue of trying to change the paradigm of mothers or grandmothers waving to their children and grandchildren in a car leaving for a perceived greater opportunity in another location."

In the aftermath of the Syracuse University debate, the Consensus question all but disappeared from the news media, leaving a void that Governor Andrew Cuomo—a supporter of consolidation—was only too happy to fill. On May 4, 2017, he signed legislation that required counties in New York to come up with a plan by September 15 that merged services, including the services of towns and villages, in order to save money. In return, he promised to match planned savings dollar for dollar with state funding, so, for example, if Onondaga County identified $50 million in savings, he'd give it that same amount of funds in a special delivery package from Albany.

Mayors and town supervisors throughout Onondaga County winced. They generally opposed any smell of consolidation or efficiency, as Murphy learned from his Consensus pitches. And they made that clear in a press conference later in the month where they stood on the steps of the county courthouse with Mayor Stephanie Miner looming over them and used words like "unfair" and "unconscionable" in reaction to Cuomo's order. They complained that Cuomo neither had given them enough time to come up with a plan nor understood that they had long tried to save money in other ways. Besides, they said, in what had become a tired mantra, the real budgetary issue in Onondaga County was state mandates.

Bolstering the old paradigm were the two major candidates vying to replace Mayor Miner, whose second term was almost up. Both opposed the "one government" solution. Democrat Juanita Williams, a self-made woman and former city hall attorney, and Independent Ben Walsh, whose father was retired Congressman Jim Walsh (and co-chair of the Consensus Commission), had channeled the growing suspicion in the city that consolidation meant disenfranchisement.[1] Even if they supported components of the plan, they neither wanted to be seen as supporting the end of city governance as we know it, nor achieve an office that could be eliminated if Consensus had its way.

As Cuomo's September deadline neared, County Executive Joanie Mahoney and other municipal leaders debated proposals that would have the county taking over groundskeeping at town and city parks and sharing various types of expensive equipment. The suburb of Fayetteville submitted a plan to consolidate courts and then withdrew it, while other villages vetoed a multitude of proposals. Miner herself scrubbed five big-ticket measures.[2]

In the end, the beleaguered committee members came up with $5 million in savings, the lion's share from bundling the purchase of supplemental health insurance for their retirees, which had been in discussion long before the talks began. It was a fraction of the tens of millions of dollars that counties such as Erie, Nassau, and Suffolk put on the table, and nobody was more disgusted than the local paper's editorial board. "If you want lower property

1. Also, candidate Walsh's grandfather William Walsh was a Syracuse mayor (1961–69) and, later, a three-term congressman.

2. Tim Knauss, "Miner Rejects Five Ideas for Shared Services," *Post-Standard,* September 12, 2017.

taxes, you should demand more of your elected officials: bolder action, tougher decisions, deeper cooperation. Syracuse will have a new mayor in January. That should be an opportunity to wipe the slate clean of old animosities and restart cooperative ventures between the city and the county."[3]

As the mayoral race intensified over accusations that candidate Williams had not played well with others during her tenure as the city's corporation counsel and had tried to intimidate Democratic voters who were getting behind Independent Walsh, there was even less discussion of consolidation. The Consensus Commission's goal to put the city-county merger on the November ballot had fizzled, meekly replaced by a proposal to unify the county's downtown jail and its suburban jail under the county sheriff's domain.

Meanwhile, Neil Murphy sallied onto the roads of Onondaga County in his pickup truck, noting municipal construction that duplicated construction in other towns. Two glistening fire departments rose in the adjoining towns of Manlius and Jamesville, he observed, knowing all the while that each of them

3. "Shared Services Plan Should Go Further," *Post-Standard,* September 14, 2017.

struggled to attract volunteer firefighters. "Now it appears that all of the towns are on a bandwagon to get a new public works barn or garage," he added. "The town of Onondaga has one that has twenty bays. But they don't have twenty trucks. I just saw where Marcellus is putting an expansion on its garage, and it sits thirty or forty feet from the state Department of Transportation garage, only separated by a large alley."

Obviously, none of this added up to the kind of forward thinking that might draw his daughter Maureen and her family back to Syracuse. But Christmas was coming and they planned to be with Murphy and his wife, Joanne, at the family vacation home. "After a few glasses of wine," he said. "I'll have a better feeling for where things stand."

Murphy's retirement, too, was written on the holiday discussion board. He planned to remain in the classroom through 2018 and maintain some consulting jobs, but leaned toward pulling away from so much community involvement. Even an offer from newly elected mayor Ben Walsh to take over Syracuse's Department of Water was rebuffed, a decision that couldn't have been easy for the area's wizard of water—until he envisioned being pulled from bed in the middle of a frigid winter's night to work another big water main break in the city.

However, water—even more than consolidation—embodied his hopes. Harking back to the days when the local salt springs birthed Syracuse's economy and the Erie Canal supercharged it, he suspected that water pointed to the city's new day. As California and the Southwest dry up, he held that water-dependent industries could flock to Upstate New York, where climate change promised to bring 20 percent more precipitation to the already soggy region. "The greatest concentration of semiconductor plants is located in Texas, Arizona, and southern California, and they need approximately 1,100 gallons of water to produce one semiconductor," he explained, as if he were in front of a classroom. "There is a company in Arizona that built a brand new tech plant, but they wind up recycling the city's waste water. It's a multi-billion-dollar plant and they spend around 100 million dollars in just managing water, recycling it. Eventually that has to catch up.

"A former colleague of mine and myself did a little study for the city of Binghamton [New York]—which is going through some tough times, too—about water. There were three clusters that we focused on, including semiconductors and the bottled water industry. We actually recommended that they identify a locator company to pitch the region to companies based on its access to water, the Susquehanna River." The point was clear: water-rich Syracuse should join the act, too. "In San Diego, treated water is selling for fourteen dollars per thousand gallons," he added. "Here in Syracuse, we spend two thirty-five for a thousand gallons."

Murphy leaned toward a bulletin board on the wall and pointed to an article he had written about the promise of the region's abundance of moisture. "Water," he murmured. "Water."

15

✧ ✧ ✧

AT HOME

Elise Baker spread the news as widely as she knew how. On a bright poster plastered on the window of her downtown floral shop and over social media, she beckoned people to her citywide prayer vigil at Kirk Park on the South Side. The recent weeks had not been kind to her, nor to the city. Since the burglary of her house in May of 2017, she had suffered another break-in and, then, the theft of her purse from her car as it sat outside her shop in the middle of the day on the city's busiest street.

But city life writ large had fared much worse. A beloved teenager named Rasheed Baker, no relation, was struck down by a bullet to the head in early June 2017, a homicide that remains unsolved as of this writing, and on Father's Day, twenty-one-year-old Khalil Howard, who had a two-year-old daughter, died in a hail of gunfire not more than a mile from Skiddy Park. Meanwhile, reports of injuries due to stabbings and shootings appeared routinely in the newspapers for an audience that may have grown numb to the out-of-control violence around them and across the nation. By July 4, it appeared that authorities had lost control of the city as a double shooting on the South Side claimed the life of one man and injured another and home-grown fireworks displays blazed unchecked all night throughout the city, their unnerving pops and explosions accentuating the mayhem in Syracuse.

Maybe it was the continued bloodshed on the South Side or her own battles with criminals that moved Elise Baker, but she gathered about fifty people in a grassy section of Kirk Park and raised her petitions to the Lord. Near the street, two men tapped on conga drums while neighbors stepped onto their porches to watch the congregation from afar. A thin woman handed out printed copies of the Lord's Prayer, and a TV station videographer set up his camera outside the ring of people that was slowly forming.

In the past fifteen months, Elise had staged at least one teen night, one poetry reading, and an open mic night, but this was the first time she took control of the evening. Usually her son, Brandon, hosted the events while she stood in the background. This night, Brandon lugged bottles of waters to the

center of the circle and tinkered with the sound system. Indeed, Elise, shining in a white pantsuit and
cap, presided over a crowd that included blacks,
whites, Hispanics, a mayoral candidate, the superintendent of city schools, and a prominent local poet
and journalist.

Then, in the cadence of an AME pastor, she un-
leashed a litany of petitions on behalf of wayward
fathers, seniors, babies, justice, peace, churches,
freedom, high-school dropouts, unity, love, the
mayor, the police, respect, responsibility, health,
the end of diabetes, the end of cancer, the end of
arthritis, youth, safe homes and neighborhoods, the
city school superintendent, judges, all present, freedom from drug addiction, the end of homelessness,
the end of gun runners, the end of pushers, foster
parents. Her appeals ended in a clatter of applause,
amens, and hallelujahs. But there was more. The
audience still in her grasp, she began to preach on
her pet concern: the absence of adult control over
rebellious children, the core plague on the city, as
she saw it. "You're scared to confront children, I
know, but if you stand up with boldness and respect and you stand in the manner of love, you can
tell those kids, 'Baby, pull your pants up, please.
I'm saying this out of love.' And once you give them
that love and they can feel it with their heart, they
will receive you most of the time. Some are going
to say something back to you. You don't have to

be scared of these kids. We raised them. They're ours. We're blaming everybody, but we have to take accountability ourselves for what we do not do with our children. Once the mother starts partying or the daddy do what he do they let the kid do what they want to at the age of twelve. The devil is alive. And if you don't chastise them, when they get downtown, they [meaning the police] are going to chastise them. So I'd rather for me to put my foot on them than for [somebody else] to kill them."

The sun fell over the trees on the west side of Kirk Park and people shuffled through the grass back to their cars and nearby homes. Elise had told them she would gauge the power of their prayer by comparing crime statistics before and after the vigil, but nobody needed such accounting. The night had a power all its own.

Back in the library where Elise frequently sat and held forth on the state of the city, she pondered her own place in it. Did Syracuse really need another community advocate and prayer warrior?

> Every day I have friends who say, "You need to start worrying about yourself and stop taking care of everybody. How can you help somebody when you're so broken down yourself?" Almost

every day I cry about that because I think we need everybody in the community to change the community. I think we can make this a better community. I moved into the community to try to help. I have never had so many sleepless nights, but thank God for the sleepless nights.

I tried to leave but my heart wouldn't go. I tried to go to Virginia, and then I started thinking about who's going to help the kids and what will my son do. I was supposed to leave in 2010, but I think about it in my head and something won't let me. I want to be free of some of the stuff, but I know until you give it to somebody else or pass it on, somebody's got to fight for that cause. If I stop, then who's going to carry it on?

I thought about me and my son and I had to make a choice. I said you can't run from the neighborhood, you've got to continue to give back. So I chose this. So since I chose it, I got to stick to it and make it work. I don't care how much peace I'll get, I'll never turn my back on it. I can't because too many people are turning their back on it.

On the Saturday before Thanksgiving of 2017, Jessi Lyons prepared the farm for its long winter's nap. She and her farm manager and a few volunteers spread mulch and dirt over quiet plots whose withered mustard greens signaled the end of the growing season. Near the shed, which had risen in the summer, hands scrambled to jumpstart a failing tractor that could speed the work along. There was reason to hurry. Snow was in the forecast and expectant clouds blanketed the sky.

While workers pulled their rakes across the ground, they chatted about the slack time ahead and who in the area might hire an under-used farmer. A recent high-school graduate looking to clock a few volunteer hours approached the scene in stunning yellow basketball shoes but sauntered away, concerned about the dirt, while a glowering neighbor with a white dog trotted past in the chill wind.

In the midst of this ritual for the season past, Jessi anticipated the season to come. If the snow held back a day or two, she commented, they could raise their high tunnels, temporary greenhouses made with heavy plastic sheeting, which would jumpstart new growth earlier next spring. And she might be able to raise a fence around the farm to keep out deer that had ravaged 25 percent of her crop during the summer and fall.

It had not been a good growing season. Aside from the hungry deer, pests such as swede midge, cabbage moths, and flea beetles had feasted on the plants, and wet weather had stunted her beloved okra. The yield of tomatoes, beans, and beets— good moneymakers normally—was minimal and gone by the end of September. "We were planning on having a decent harvest to sell this November, but we don't have anything now," she complained.

Worse than that was the struggle to attract and maintain a workforce. Sadly, Terrence Newley, the young man who seemed to love farming and see a future in it, never learned computer programs or improved his communication skills as Jessi had wished. Nor had he learned to drive, even after she arranged for his road classes.

> I drove with him once and it was so scary. He had given me lots of assurances that he knew how to drive. Clearly, he had only driven a few times and we went on the freeway and he was petrified, so he has a lot of self-confidence but not a lot of context, so when he thinks he can drive, he doesn't know what it means to drive regularly, so he did not pass his driver's test.
>
> And he didn't follow up on the other things that I needed him to do. He was going through a lot. He was trying to get custody of his children, so he had all this legal stuff happen. There were some other personal things involving his kids' mom. He had made some bad choices. He was supposed to be in a role of mentoring young people who volunteered on the farm, and I had to make the decision that he wasn't fit to be a role model. He was just clearly not making good decisions and they

were personal decisions but when it meant that he couldn't show up for work for a couple of days that was a problem. That was really hard. I ended up feeling really bad because he'd say things like, "You just want to make me a slave." Showing up to work on time and not being on your phone when you're working is reasonable.

The bigger lesson—and it's not specific to Terrence—is we really wanted to hire people from our community and use this as an opportunity for skill development, and I was very naïve about how hard it is to do workforce development, especially in communities that have high illiteracy rates and extreme poverty and the trauma that comes with poverty. There's just a lot more to it than to just teach somebody how to do a thing. It's things like childcare and transportation and all those logistical things that make it possible for somebody to be just an employee that I take for granted. It's just an assumption that you have to take care of those things to be a functional employee and, of course, if you have no money, it's very hard to do those things to get a job, to find transportation, to find a sitter.

After Terrence departed, the farm hired an immigrant from an African country who knew how to farm. Jessi and her farm manager, Alice, relaxed as they watched him intuitively gauge soil balance and the ripeness of vegetables and fruits. He was a godsend, until he wasn't. "He tried to kiss me," said Jessi. "And then he groped Alice. And we told him to leave and then he kept coming back. You have no idea how frustrating that was. Like, really? We finally find somebody who's competent. Why did he have to do that? Why?"

The disappointing employees put the farm directly at odds with the goals of the Brady Faith Center, her sponsor. Obviously, Jessi was supposed to encourage workforce development with an eye on improving lives and community. But how could the farm achieve those ends if it failed to sow and grow and harvest? She had three more years remaining in the five-year commitment from her patron who had funded almost everything, so she had to focus on making the farm work. Which meant workforce development received less of her brainpower. "Right now I'm trying to master too many things at once and that's preventing us from doing a good job in the things that we need to do to farm," she said. "We have to make those compromises and it's just so hard because in our community what it looks like is an important thing."

In farming, as in baseball, there's always next year, so Jessi put to rest her beds and reached out to a few young men she'd met in the neighborhood who work in landscaping and could transfer those skills to the dream of urban agriculture.

When the snow finally came, she carried her satchel of seeds to the nearby Southside Academy Charter School, where she had many little friends who in better weather often scampered across the street to visit the farm. "There's a handful of those kids who desperately want more of it. They like thinking about it, the physical nature of it, they like being outside, they like us, they like the warm environment we created. We are now normalizing this idea of growing food in an urban place. This idea of being outside and doing physical work is not a weird thing. It's part of an expectation of civilization, and so now we have exposed them to it. That's the long view."

It was two days before Christmas in a sub shop all yellow and brown. While heavy snowflakes pelted the windows, seasonal music that had become cloying at this late hour blared from the in-store speakers. At the counter, Justo Triana ordered his first cheese steak in America.

A lot had happened to him since the early autumn. After another flying visit to his family in late August, he had found a new afternoon teaching job in the city with the new title of "instructor," and he prepared to submit the graduate school applications that could revive the academic career he had left behind in Cuba. He performed impressively on the GRE and even better on the TOEFL, the test that gauges English-language abilities.

Meanwhile, dark circles scored the skin below his eyes and his hair loss accelerated. So he relented and moved his overnight janitorial shift at Upstate Hospital to evening shifts on the weekends, even if it meant giving up his health coverage now that he'd be working less than half time. "What is the point of having health insurance versus not having health insurance and being healthy? So I prefer to go to the market and pay two, maybe three, hundred monthly and be in better physical shape because this has been killing me," he said.

In the midst of these shifting winds, his spirit weathered another blow: the further delay of his family's deliverance to Syracuse. In late September, personnel in the US Embassy in Havana had fallen ill after "sonic attacks," which President Trump blamed on the Cuban government. Like almost everything else that had come out of the new administration, the whole thing seemed torn from a science-fiction comic book. But Justo watched crestfallen as the Department of State removed dozens of embassy personnel from Cuba, including the staffers that were supposed to interview his family as part of the relocation process.

The interview was the second-to-last step, and now his wife and two children would have to take that step in Georgetown, Guyana, where some US officials had relocated, costing Justo more in travel expenses. From the beginning, he had expected them to arrive in the spring of 2017, but now he'd be lucky if he saw them in the spring of 2020.

"My wife's really concerned," he explained. "She's alone and she's dealing with the two children and her mother and my mother, too, so it's hard for her trying to keep things running. My son is sixteen and is military able now. That could be a problem. If the visa process continues to drag, they could retain him for service. They can draft him."

While the snow piled up outside the sub shop and cars crawled by on the nearby road, Justo turned to his adopted hometown. "I like the city of Syracuse. It's not Miami, but I don't like Miami. I wanted to experience the real American culture and going to Florida is just a non-communist Cuba. But I think Syracuse is fine.

"I feel safe here," he continued.

I have my network of friends. Not too many but just a few and that's enough. I don't like to begin again in another city and begin to start moving up from the beginning and try to build relationships and to try to get a good job. I know this city. I know some places that I can go and the best ways to get there. I know the school system. I know the hospitals. So I think it's a safe move for me and my family.

I was even talking with my wife yesterday about the weather here. In Cuba there's only one summer all the year round and there's a dry season and a rainy season. Here you have to deal with the snow and the rain and all this weather differences. It makes you tougher. I think at some point the geography makes a man. The meridional countries tend to be soft on people because you don't have to deal with anything. You can get drunk and stay overnight laying on the street and you'll be fine the next day. But here you have to plan ahead, to work with the elements. You have to deal with them. And that makes you tougher. And that's fine. I can't wait to see my son shoveling the snow on the driveway. It's going to be amazing.

On the other hand, I would like to see a Syracuse with less violence, less drugs. I would like to see some improvement with the housing and the communities that are affected, especially the South Side, the West Side, the North Side. I think that the schools are trying at their maximum capacity and I think that the only source of improvement would be the economy, to try to boost the economy in some way to create more jobs and to give more opportunities for people to improve their lives in an honest way. That would be a wonderful city to live in.

I am not optimistic but neither am I pessimistic. We'll have to wait and see what's going on.

I like the fact that Syracuse is not a conservative city and it's not a liberal city. It's an independent city. And the people of Syracuse are sensitive to this refugee thing. If we compare Syracuse to Alabama or Virginia or Texas, maybe we have a big advancement when it comes to relationships between different nationalities. And that's a big plus. I think we have the human drive. It's here. We only need to get it to move, to let that human potential happen.

The human customers had stayed away from the sub shop during the evening, wary of the snowstorm, and now the store approached closing time and the last Christmas carol. Balling up the sandwich wrapping in front of him, Justo pulled out one of the themes from the disembodied holiday songs.

It's because of hope that I'm here. I was trying to fulfill my dreams to experience freedom, to be able to think in the way you want, to speak in the way you want, and to be able to build your future and raise your family in an honest way, respecting all others and being respected. I think that's my hope and it's driven me all my life.

Hope is what makes you move forward. It's like a magnet to your improvement. If you don't have hope, if you don't have a dream, if you don't have a goal, you're not a human being. You're just an animal. That's why addiction is so dangerous, because the moment that you don't have hope, you're done. You stop living.

In these days, we think despair overshadows hope. But actually there's always been the same amount of hope and despair. The thing is we have to build hope, move towards hope. That's what will improve the situation. If we go back in history a couple of hundred years ago there was slavery and people were profiting off slavery and now we're better. Thirty years ago, we were on the verge of a nuclear catastrophe and we were able to move forward. And now there is the same amount of problems and hope. This is what we're able to see and experience. In the future, our children will say the same: "I struggle to see hope, but I think we in the long run are moving towards hope."

In the early months of 2018 so much in the Syracuse zone remained uncertain, both in the lives of individuals portrayed here and in the city itself. The new mayor, Ben Walsh, entertained some regional consolidation but took no decisive steps in that direction, while Donald Trump continued to keep refugees on edge and disrupt the national and international terrain. In Skiddy Park, a police substation had opened in a small renovated building in hopes of improving community-police relations, but dozens of bullets had pocked the outside walls and shatterproof windows. Stephanie Miner retreated to private life after two terms as mayor, unsure of whether or not to run for governor or the US Congress and with little chance of winning either.

Ted and Willa Hoston's vision of themselves in Syracuse must have shone like morning sunlight while they motored east across the flat Midwest in the late 1940s, but their grandson Stefon Greene's place in the city seemed murky as the new year dawned. Certainly, he had picked up the cord of life that his mother had let go of decades before, resurrecting in his own particular lineage his grandparents' estimation of Syracuse's promise. But where, he asked, did the city figure in the promises he made to himself?

Recalling protagonists in great works by African American writers like Richard Wright, Ralph Ellison, and James Baldwin, Stefon found himself between two worlds, transcending tragic elements of the city's South Side but not quite trusting the middle class's extended hand. "There's one particular piece of literature that opened the door: *Narrative of the Life of Frederick Douglass*," he explained.

Douglass says when he learned to read that he realized then he wasn't like the other slaves, but he still wasn't like the white people. That was the first time that I read or learned that this was a feeling that I was also having. It was a conscious decision for me to say, "I don't want to be like everything else I know and I have to be something different." Selling drugs and being in the streets wasn't for me, it wasn't my character type. As much as I tried to adhere to it or be like my uncles and be like people in my life that I know that live like this, I really couldn't. I had to consciously tell myself that I was going to go to school and do all those things. I feel like I ostracized myself from some of my friends. My closest friends, I'm still really close to. They're proud of me. But I do find myself not talking about certain things around them. I don't want them to feel like I'm better than them. It's weird that being black in America you want to be just as good and you want to feel equal but at the same time you don't want to feel better than other black people and you don't want other black people thinking that you're better than them. It's something that my grandmother used to say, "It's being an uppity nigger." It's a harsh term to use but it's something that's been around a long time, before me.

A selfish part of it is wanting to brag about what you do, feel proud of it. I'm lucky enough to have close friends to tell about the television station. I want to brag about those things. But I also want to educate. As a young black man, it's not only good to show young people that there's more out there than basketball or football or rapping, it's a responsibility. It's an obligation when people need me to speak somewhere or do anything to help young black men. It's literally an obligation as a young black professional. It's also an obligation and a responsibility to do things outside of that, to not cheat on my wife, to not do the things that we're so known for, to not be angry, to not to do those things. You got to show people who are younger than you that it's okay to want to go to school, it's okay to want to have to have an education. It's okay to do things that people don't think you should be doing, like wanting to be a filmmaker or an artist.

I don't like when people say, "I'm so proud that you went to college and are working as a TV producer." That's what people are supposed to do. People are supposed to graduate from high school and go to college and get jobs and live happy lives. It's not supposed to be surprising that I do those things. I hate living with that stigma that you're young and black and you're not a basketball player and you're not in jail and you're not selling drugs. Good job? I'm just doing what people are supposed to do.

But I feel like I have to reach the height of my potential while I'm young enough to do it and I have enough energy. To do that, I have to leave Syracuse. You have to see more of the world and you have to know it. I blamed a lot of not wanting to go away for college to feeling like I wasn't good enough. That was forty percent of it. Sixty percent of it was I was born and raised in Syracuse and I got homesick before I even left. I couldn't imagine leaving home. Now, being twenty-nine, I feel like it was for the better to stay. I feel like I had better life experiences. I feel like I built up a way better work ethic, and I got to marry the love of my life. That also would have been at a time when my mother got clean. I wouldn't have seen that. I got to see her in a new light that I never, ever in my life saw her in. I may have missed all that. I may have been more disconnected from here if I had went away to school. I care about where I'm from. I said that in my job interview at the station: "I care about this city."

Would I raise a family in Syracuse? Of course I would. Would I retire in Syracuse? Of course I would. Would I buy a ridiculously big house on the South Side that's ridiculously cheap in a bad neighborhood? I would because it's the neighborhood I know. But I couldn't see myself living with the regret of not trying to be something more. My ideal would be to go away from Syracuse and become a movie director and come back and buy a huge house in Sedgwick . . . a nice neighborhood. I've never known anybody who lived in Sedgwick. But I would love to do that. I'd be home. And I'd be in Syracuse.

EPILOGUE

✧ ✧ ✧

STILL ON
THE EDGE

The evening situation on Harrison Street near Elizabeth Blackwell Street in Syracuse will tell you a lot about the city. Cars and pickup trucks driven by workers at Syracuse University and several nearby hospitals pour onto the roadway and jockey for the right-hand lanes that will take them to an elevated portion of Interstate 81 and then to the northern, western, and eastern suburbs. Winking at passersby is the old Washington Irving School, once the bulwark of the 15th Ward, whose houses and businesses fell to bulldozers in the 1960s to make room for the much-disputed superhighway.

These days the federal-style building houses the school district headquarters, but it also reminds

Syracusans of the city that urban renewal left behind, while Elizabeth Blackwell Street, named for the first woman in America to receive a medical degree, recalls the city's progressive past. But the blinking vehicles take little notice. Traffic lurches to the right, leaving two empty lanes on the left that point to downtown and, beyond that, to the worried South Side.

A rusted, hulking structure, I-81 gives commuters an easy way to live the benefits of the city—jobs, courts, restaurants, entertainment—without having to live there or give much thought to the urban pathology. Even more worrisome, the looming highway demoralizes the people who must live in its shadow, particularly some residents of the Pioneer Homes, whose rooftops nearly touch the skyway.

But even the Berlin Wall came down. And in 2020 there was hope that the state would raze the I-81 viaduct, making way for mixed-use development in the spirit of the old 15th Ward, a potential statement in a city that knows few big statements that are meaningful.

Cities in search of another epochal moment, such as Rochester, Milwaukee, New Haven, Chattanooga, and Charlotte, have either torn down highways that gutted their downtowns or plan to do so soon. It's an undeniable juggernaut fueled by evolving notions about urban living, the aging of federal highways, and studies that show Americans are driving less. But, although the New York State Department of Transportation has concluded that the stretch of highway that runs through the city should be rerouted, stern opposition in suburbia and among some downtown merchants has aligned against such plans.

Could a big, transformative moment be sailing past Syracuse? It wouldn't be the first time.

The Consensus Commission's final report, issued in 2017, pointed to a new day in which reimagined local government could facilitate prosperity in the Syracuse region. But in 2020 nobody in politics mentioned regional consolidation anymore despite co-director Neil Murphy's unflagging belief that the plan would eventually take hold. News organizations dropped the story, and the county executive, who had replaced Consensus advocate Joanie Mahoney and moved to the suburbs after building a political base in the city, showed no signs of dropping the opposition to consolidation efforts that he had exhibited in his former job in the county legislature. In the city, Mayor Ben Walsh had chosen not to embrace broad regional cooperation.

And still Syracuse waited for a big idea.

In the late spring of 2019, the city glumly returned to the scene of the first chapter of this book: Skiddy

Park. Police had pulled over a car nearby that was blaring ear-splitting music. No question, insanely loud music served up by drivers "bumping their system" ranks high among the city nuisances, waking you in the middle of a summer's night, rattling your bedroom windows like a bomb blast. But few victims of such noise would endorse the police's response on Friday, May 31.

Because violating the city noise ordinance is an arrestable offense or the driver Shaolin Moore was a known troublemaker, the police, just off a drug bust in the park, might have seen an opportunity to search the car, so they asked Moore to exit his vehicle. But when Moore refused, Officer Christopher Buske pulled him from his car, tackled him, punched him twice, and pinned his head to the ground. Later Buske claimed he saw Moore reach for his pocket, which was true, although he was trying to get to his phone. Not surprisingly, video shot by Moore's passenger went viral.

Watching at home, Stefon Greene just shook his head. There was nothing new here; he'd seen or heard of dozens of similar encounters with police. But, in the past, when police had pulled him over for noise, they had merely issued a ticket. Indeed, the police reaction to Moore's resistance may have been typical, but as the age of cellphone video has proven, violent arrests make for poor optics. "It rarely looks clean or good and takes place under intense

STILL ON THE EDGE 255

circumstances," said Kenton Buckner, the city's new police chief, at a press conference two weeks later.[1]

In the wake of the video release, protesters descended on city hall, and the NAACP demanded police evidence associated with the arrest. On the South Side, Elise Baker couldn't believe her eyes, taking to Facebook to complain that Moore clearly was not resisting arrest and a white driver would have been greeted differently. Faintly echoing Elise, Mayor Walsh, standing next to Buckner at the press conference, telegraphed his understanding of how the video moment could breed suspicion. "We have much more to do to ultimately create a climate of trust and mutual support for our officers and our community. It will be painful at times but the relationship between police and the community is strained and it must be healed."

It was a high point for the new mayor, who had appeared at the press conference in support of his chief, the force, and the law while acknowledging between the lines that the Moore incident shouldn't have gone down as it did. Albeit indirectly, he had

1. Chris Baker, "Council Head: Why Was the Officer So Angry," *Post-Standard,* June 5, 2019; "Police Officers Disciplined for Behavior During Loud Music Arrest; Use of Force Deemed Appropriate," updated June 18, 2019, https://www.localsyr.com/news/local-news/police-officers-disciplined-for-behavior-during-loud-music-arrest-use-of-force-deemed-appropriate/.

put his finger on one of the city's desperate conflicts. But his words were soon forgotten and the glare on police intensified when, a few days later, a Syracuse police officer shot and mortally wounded a seventy-four-year-old man on the South Side who had waved at them what police later said was a starter pistol used at track meets, while, at the same time, a trial proceeded that would award $35,000 to a twenty-five-year-old black man who'd been beaten up by a Syracuse police officer in a 2014 arrest.

Were these cases a matter of defective policing or was the populace of Syracuse running amok? Either way, the incidents were neither encouraging potential new residents to choose Syracuse nor giving current citizens who feared police brutality a reason to stay.

The old town inched closer to the edge.

But could it still pull back?

The answer may be in the five primary individuals profiled in this book who haven't followed the ramp to the I-81 viaduct, making the all-important choice to stay and make life work for themselves. A diverse group, they fortify the city in concrete ways—paying taxes, reclaiming abandoned tracts of land, improving language skills of lifeblood immigrants. But the ideals they exhibit may be more vital:

caring for people around them, sacrificing in service of the greater good, stirring community spirit and cohesion. In one carefully wrapped bundle, seemingly small contributions can add up to success where mayors, city councilors, county executives, governors, and presidents have mostly failed.

This writer set out to take the temperature of Syracuse by chronicling everyday citizens, acknowledging that only a multiplicity of views can produce anything close to an accurate reading. But along the way, he grew to believe that Neil Murphy, Justo Triana, Jessi Lyons, Elise Baker, and Stefon Greene represent major roles on the urban stage that must be played if the city is to thrive.

Although regional consolidation has stalled, Murphy represents enlightened civic leadership from which the long view, systemic change, and innovative thinking must emerge. There's a poverty of such leadership in Syracuse, but Murphy's work on behalf of transformative government and other issues offers hope that unselfish, visionary leadership can live in the region. In 2020, he's well past retirement age with no plans yet to break camp in Syracuse, despite his earlier predictions of a 2018 retirement. And he stays busy on projects like a center of excellence on the question of safe water. His long commitment to clean water, the growth of SUNY-ESF, and regional cooperation slowed the city's progression toward the edge, a valuable legacy.

Less than a mile from Murphy's office, Justo Triana (now a US citizen) has purchased a house for his family, who finally arrived from Cuba in late 2019. Like his fellow immigrants, he embodies the building blocks that the stonecutters of the urban epoch scatter throughout a city. A throwback to earlier decades when Irish and Italians and sojourners like Ted and Willa Hoston arrived in Syracuse, he bears down on his daily tasks in order to eke out a living and claim his place as a teacher and a scholar in the city's preparation economy. Endowed with a critical mass of people like Justo who bring essential skills and fresh perspectives and whose primary goal is familial stability, a city like Syracuse can thrive.

In a sense, Jessi Lyons epitomizes the space between the Triana and Murphy archetypes: the newcomer who wants something as modest as a home for her family and yet seeks to bend the city to her big vision. The Portland native and her husband have bought that home, no small victory for a city that is ranked seventeenth in the nation for the highest percentage of homeowners who leave and never return, as she aspires to create a new model of food production and consumption for the people.[2] Where she first gazed on a vacant lot known

2. Esther Trattner, "People Can't Flee These U.S. Cities Fast Enough," posted March 3, 2019, https://moneywise.com /a/people-cant-flee-these-us-cities-fast-enough.

for violent criminal activity, she now sees a happily disheveled farm whose produce travels to plates and bowls throughout the region while enriching the local employment pool.

And, finally, all praise for those who personify the bedrock of the Syracuse community, believing that the city is their destiny: Elise Baker, shepherdess of the people, Stefon Greene, the only native Syracusan in this story, and others like them whose parents and grandparents built Syracuse. In a sense, they feel duty-bound to redeem their forebears' choice to settle in the city, and, while others come and go, they keep the lantern burning for generation after generation. As long as they stay, optimism abides and the chance for a renewed vision endures.

As essential ingredients in a recipe for rejuvenation, the Syracuse Five, and even public character number one Trevor Russell, represent a dream for the city: yes, a rolling path away from oblivion and back into the national sunlight. But ingredients must be collected and deployed for the long-term good. Who or what will do that? There is no answer right now. Only hope.

Not surprisingly, Stefon finally left the television station, fed up with the mind games and fickle administrative maneuvering. But he remains in the city.

As does Elise. She has clung to her small patch of downtown, the forever-struggling flower shop, and she keeps an eye on police–community encounters and the flock that marches daily by her store. Lately on social media, she has railed against Trump, his wall, and the stench from a clogged sewer line in her neighborhood. Soon it will be time for another dance fest for the kids and a South Side prayer vigil. But before she begins, she paused the other day and logged on to her Facebook page. "Good night, world," she wrote. "Sweet dreams."

SELECTED
BIBLIOGRAPHY

Bernstein, Peter L. *Wedding of the Waters: The Erie Canal and the Making of a Great Nation*. New York: W.W. Norton, 2005.

Binelli, Mark. *Detroit City Is the Place to Be: The Afterlife of an American Metropolis*. New York: Picador, 2013.

Case, Dick. *Remembering Syracuse*. Charleston, SC: The History Press, 2009.

Chase, Franklin. *Syracuse and Its Environs: A History*, Vols. 1–3. New York: Lewis Historical Publishing Company, 1924.

Clarke, Susan E., and Gary L. Gaile. *The Work of Cities*. Minneapolis: University Press of Minnesota, 1998.

Connors, Dennis J. *Crossroads in Time: An Illustrated History of Syracuse*. Syracuse: Onondaga Historical Association, 2006.

Ducre, K. Animashaun. *A Place We Call Home: Race and Justice in Syracuse*. Syracuse, NY: Syracuse University Press, 2012.

Duneier, Mitchell. *Sidewalk*. New York: Farrar, Straus and Giroux, 1999.

Gans, Herbert J. *The Urban Villagers: Group and Class in the Life of Italian-Americans*. New York: The Free Press, 1982 (originally published in 1962).

Gessen, Keith, and Stephen Squibb, eds. *City by City: Dispatches from the American Metropolis*. New York: n+1/Farrar, Straus and Giroux, 2015.

Giffels, David. *The Hard Way on Purpose: Essays and Dispatches from the Rust Belt*. New York: Scribner, 2014.

Hardin, Evamaria. *Syracuse Landmarks: An AIA Guide to Downtown and Historic Neighborhoods*. Syracuse: Onondaga Historical Association/Syracuse University Press, 1993.

Kirst, Sean. *The Soul of Central New York*. Syracuse: Syracuse University Press, 2016.

LeDuff, Charlie. *Detroit: An American Autopsy*. New York: Penguin Books, 2014.

Marc, David. *Leveling the Playing Field: The Story of the Syracuse 8*. Syracuse: Syracuse University Press, 2015.

Marshall, Alex. *How Cities Work: Suburbs, Sprawl, and the Roads Not Taken*. Austin: University of Texas Press, 2000.

Munson, Lillian Steele. *Syracuse: The City that Salt Built*. New York: Pageant Press International, 1969.

Rudolph, B.G. *From a Minyan to a Community: A History of the Jews of Syracuse*. Syracuse, NY: Syracuse University Press, 1970.

Russo, Richard. *Elsewhere: A Memoir*. New York: Vintage, 2013.

Sheriff, Carol. *The Artificial River: The Erie Canal and the Paradox of Progress, 1817–1862*. New York: Hill and Wang, 1997.

Smith, H.P., and Robert Joki, ed. *Syracuse and Its Surroundings: A Victorian Photo Tour of New York's Salt City.* Hensonville, NY: Black Dome Press, 2002.

Stamps, S. David, and Miriam Burney Stamps. *Salt City and Its Black Community: A Sociological Study of Syracuse, New York.* Syracuse, NY: Syracuse University Press, 2008.

Storey, Mike. *Heartland: A Natural History of Onondaga County, NY.* Syracuse, NY: Onondaga Audubon Society, 1977.

INDEX